LIVE AT THE FILLMORE EAST
A PHOTOGRAPHIC MEMOIR

Photography by Amalie R. Rothschild

Text by Amalie R. Rothschild
with Ruth Ellen Gruber

THUNDER'S
MOUTH
PRESS

Published by
    Thunder's Mouth Press
    An Imprint of Avalon Publishing Group Incorporated
    161 William Street, 16th Floor
    New York, New York 10038

The names and marks:
"The Fillmore East," "The Fillmore," "Live at the Fillmore," "Fillmore West," "The Fillmore Auditorium" are the property of Bill Graham Enterprises, Inc., a California Corporation doing business as Bill Graham Presents and are used with permission.

Library of Congress Catalog Card Number: 99-65654

Cloth edition ISBN: 1-56025-244-8
Paperback edition ISBN: 1-56025-279-0

Cover design: Howard Grossman 12E Design

An Acid Test Productions book

Printed in China through QuinnEssentials Books and Printing, Inc.

Distributed by
    Publishers Group West
    1700 Fourth Street
    Berkeley, CA 94710
    510.528.1444

Amalie R. Rothschild's prints are available through
    SoHo Triad Fine Arts Gallery
    107 Grand Street
    New York, NY 10013
    212.965.9500 Sohotriad@msn.com

Amalie R. Rothschild can be reached at A.Rothschild@agora.stm.it

CONTENTS

This book is dedicated to Bill Graham and everyone who ever worked at the Fillmore East.

The crowd for Crosby, Stills, Nash and Young tickets, May 1970. I had my studio in one of the loft spaces upstairs in the theater building, so I was usually around during the day, as well. It was a revelation when so many people showed up on a warm May day to wait for the box office to open to sell C,S,N &Y tickets. It was the first time a crowd that big had gathered – a moment worth documenting. It took me some time, but I eventually found someone who let me into the building catty-corner across the street and allowed me to go up to the roof to get the picture.

FOREWORD by MICKEY HART

The Fillmore East was a unique venue, one of the few places the Grateful Dead would play in New York. Amalie R. Rothschild's pictures bring back the entire F.E. experience in vivid detail.

There's no way to talk about the Fillmore East, though, without talking about Bill Graham. Bill put tremendous effort into

everything he did. He wanted to be the best – the best basketball player one-on-one, the best promoter, the best judge of what the people in his audiences would love to see. It was this "best thing" that was his strength. This was the root of the passion that he brought to everything he did, and this is what made his Fillmores so special. Even arranging the tables and chairs, putting flowers in the dressing rooms, making everything ready before

the people were let in to a concert, all this was done with a super, almost obsessive concentration. Musicians felt this energy when they played for Bill Graham. That's why the bands would deliver once-in-a-lifetime performances.

Bill believed in magic, and magic was the key component at the Fillmore East. Indeed, by day the F.E. looked like an innocuous, plain building sitting on the corner of a typical street in the East Village. But at night it came alive. The building became a living organism – breathing, pulsating, vibrating, swaying with the emotional outpouring from within. It became a sacred space: a cathedral of sound consecrated by the testimony of the extraordinary performances that took place there. Bill called it a Palace of Sound. People came with great expectations, and trance and ecstasy, ritual and rapture were courted. The Fillmore East was the church of rock and roll, and Bill was the shepherd tending the flock.

Bill shuttled back and forth cross-country between the Fillmore West and the Fillmore East, sometimes twice in one week. He brought the West Coast experience to New York, but the East Coast energy was quite different from that in San Francisco, more frenzied. There was a greater hunger for the music in New York: The music had broken out on the West Coast and the East was trying to catch up.

The Fillmore East had lights, sounds, and a smell – musty, like a gymnasium – that all added to the particular chemistry. It was small enough that you could hear the room. You could hear the walls, you could hear the music coming back to you. The F.E. had a unique sound – I could recognize it. It was a good sounding space, not too big, not too small, kind of intimate. And the audiences were over-the-top.

My favorite memories of the Fillmore East are playing all night. There was no curfew – the second shows were the best and we could go on and on until dawn. And every night the part we loved most was when Bill Graham begged us for an encore. He would beg us. He would give us money, blow us kisses, stand on his head. He would do handstands. "They're tearing my place apart, listen to them, they're ripping up the seats. Play one more song."

"Sorry, Bill," we'd say, "we've given it all we've got."

"Come on, they're ripping my seats!"

We'd egg him on until he'd do something crazy to get the encore out of us: "Okay, Bill, recite 'Mary had a Little Lamb.'" And he'd recite it!

Rock and roll was a baby back then and Bill Graham was its midwife – he birthed the modern version of a rock and roll concert. He used to say to me, "If you give somebody a diamond and you put it in a plain brown wrapper, they won't know its worth. But if you take something good and package it well, people will know that it is of great value." He had the vision that a rock concert should be more than just listening to music. So he dressed it up -- he put a dress on rock and roll. He thought of rock as grand opera.

Bill also knew how to harness the energy of rock and make it a business. The Grateful Dead and the other bands couldn't do that; Grateful Dead energy was made in chaos – we'd laugh at Bill trying to organize us. We'd watch him kick and scream – we never took him seriously. He'd come about an inch from your eyeball as if he was going to eat your head and scream at you. When it was over we'd laugh about it. We'd say "Okay Bill, you've got five minutes to go crazy. Okay Bill, your five minutes are up." Yet, it was Bill who stepped in and made it work; he was the only person with a clipboard. He saw us musicians as deviants, wayward children irresponsible in the ways of business. We were transients, and he felt it was his responsibility to create a home for us. He was the wiser older brother whose mission was to make a safe haven for the reckless, carefree spirit of rock and roll.

For a few short, memorable years, the Fillmore East was where we played it best.

The Grateful Dead at Fillmore East, February 14, 1970.

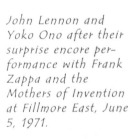

John Lennon and Yoko Ono after their surprise encore performance with Frank Zappa and the Mothers of Invention at Fillmore East, June 5, 1971.

THE CRADLE OF ROCK

This book is a labor of love: love of an era, love of a lifestyle, love of music, and love of a group of people whose extraordinary creative energy came together at the end of the 1960s in a blaze of innovation that paved the way for the multimedia presentation of music now so embedded in popular culture.

For more than two years, between 1969 and 1971, I was the unofficial house photographer at the Fillmore East, the legendary rock venue located in a rundown former movie house at 6th Street and Second Avenue in New York's East Village. Opened in March 1968 by the flamboyant counterculture impresario Bill Graham as the East Coast anchor of his San Francisco-based Fillmore operation, the F.E. claimed a unique place in the rock scene of the psychedelic '60s.

The F.E. show list was a Who's Who of the rock revolution: The Jefferson Airplane, Jimi Hendrix, Janis Joplin, Ike and Tina Turner, The Grateful Dead, The Who, Country Joe and the Fish, Richie Havens, Chuck Berry, Elton John, Crosby, Stills and Nash (with and without Young) — and dozens more. Everyone who was anyone played there. The only notable exceptions were the Rolling Stones, Bob Dylan and the Beatles — but some of these artists, too, including Dylan, would attend shows at the Fillmore East as spectators, usually watching from VIP guest seating in the sound booth. One of the most memorable moments I witnessed at the F.E. came in June 1971 at the tail end of a Frank Zappa and the Mothers of Invention concert. At about two in the morning, unannounced, John Lennon and Yoko Ono left the sound booth where they had been watching the concert and joined the Mothers onstage for a surprise encore. It lasted at least half an hour, a very idiosyncratic improv of two songs — "I Love You Baby, Please Don't Go" and "Scumbag" — during which two of the Mothers actually swooped in and completely covered Yoko Ono with a big burlap bag, microphone and all, as she was singing.

But the Fillmore East was much more than great acts and great sounds. It was the place where rock music became rock theater.

The F.E. setting was part of what made it unique. With its ponderous, 1920s-style movie palace trappings, including Corinthian columns, a grand proscenium arch, ornate painted murals, and even an artificial gilt chandelier, the Fillmore exuded an exotic sense of faded grandeur. What's more, it was a real theater, where people had to sit in reserved seats and actually listen to the music and watch the stage effects — not a ballroom, open-air stage, gymnasium or club with a floor, where fans could mill around, smoke dope, go into a trance or dance during the shows. (Not that they didn't try, of course — countless F.E. seats had their springs ruined by people jumping up on them and jiving.)

This was a radical idea at the time. It formalized the rock experience into a theatrical event. Not only did this force the audience to focus on the stage show, but the artists, in turn, were forced to play to the audience rather than, as sometimes happened, to themselves. This dynamic placed new demands on lighting and sound technology, too. The tech crew rose to the challenge, creating systems that became standards in the industry. Ironically, the F.E.'s innovations helped hasten the theater's demise: The presentation of rock concerts became a visual and musical art form so successful that it soon outgrew the 2600-seat Fillmore, evolving into the stadium concert phenomenon of today, as well as the ubiquitous mix of sound and image we find in music videos, advertising, film and even fashion.

From April 1969 until the F.E.'s marathon final concert on June 27, 1971, I was privileged to have total access to the Fillmore East: out front, backstage, in the wings, and in the inner sanctums of sound and light production. I wandered at will with two Nikon Fs — one for color and one for black & white — and a set of seven lenses, photographing whatever I found interesting, exciting or even just fun. In all, I shot about 20,000 pictures documenting every facet of the F.E.'s day-to-day operations: vibrant onstage performances by the top rock acts of the era; backstage banter; bleary-eyed breakfasts after the shows at Ratner's, a famous kosher dairy restaurant right next door that was open 24 hours. I also captured behind-the-scenes shots of tech crews at work, light shows in action, ticket sellers, management offices and, of course, the fans. The fans who camped outside for tickets, the fans who crowded the red plush seats that climbed upward through two balconies, the fans who vamped in the aisles, and the fans who simply hung around outside under the glowing Fillmore marquee in order to see and be seen at the ground-zero of rock.

I'll never forget the first time I walked into the F.E. It was on a Friday evening in 1968, not long after Bill Graham had transformed the seedy old Loew's Commodore into New York's most exciting rock venue. In the few short years since he had begun promoting rock concerts in San

Amalie in the light show dressing room backstage working with film loops.

Francisco at the original Fillmore Auditorium and then the Carousel Ballroom which he renamed the Fillmore West, Graham had become a figure of almost mythical proportions on the music scene. A Berlin-born Holocaust survivor who fled to the U.S. as a child during World War II and lost his parents in the Nazi death camps, Graham was a would-be actor who turned to concert promotion just as the counterculture explosion was taking off. He was famous not just for his musical savvy but for his workaholic compulsion, his towering temper — and, importantly, for the personal attention he gave to performers and to making each show a success. His own experience of hardship also contributed to a social conscience: Graham opened the Fillmore to benefits for liberal causes and to charitable activities such as a Christmas toy drive for underprivileged children. He even once arranged for a doctor to come and give all F.E. staffers flu shots!

A PR release once called the F.E. "a pleasure dome for the young, the hip, and the brave." I was certainly young when I first walked though the door — 22 — but I didn't consider myself particularly hip, and my bravery was the bravery of youth, the '60s and the art and filmmaking scene to which I belonged. I had serious, soulful eyes and long dark hair down to my waist, and there's hardly a picture of me from those days in which I'm smiling. At the time, I was a graduate film student at New York University. Our building, as well as the rest of the NYU School of the Arts, stood next door to the building housing the F.E. The NYU environment was bursting with intellectual ferment and creative energy. When Graham arrived to establish the F.E., it was natural that he recruited the bulk of his technical team from students and staff at NYU. I was fascinated by the technical as well as the artistic aspects of filmmaking, and some of the people Graham hired were my close friends. These included Lee Osborne, an NYU audio engineer and film equipment technician, who became the Fillmore East's first sound engineer. Lee gave me my first F.E. pass for a concert.

I turned up early, so that Lee could show me the technical layout of the theater — the stage, the lights, backstage, everywhere. From down in the orchestra section, he pointed out the sound booth, which occupied the right-hand box above the stage. I looked up and did a double take. Prominently displayed on the sound booth wall was a poster — a poster that I had designed for a student project. Seeing my own work hanging there, waiting for me, triggered a sensation of deja vu. I felt that my spirit, or my artistic sensibilities, had somehow preceded my physical entrance into the Fillmore East embrace. I knew that the F.E. was where I belonged.

From that moment on, I spent as much time as I could at the theater, obtaining passes for concerts and getting to know the staff and the artistic routine. It was not until a year later, however, that I began dedicating myself to creating a photographic documentation. The turning point came in April 1969, when F.E. House Manager Jerry Pompili caught me trying to sneak a friend in on my own guest pass and threw me off the premises, forbidding me to return. With a shock, I realized that I couldn't bear the thought of never being able to go to the Fillmore again. I knew I had to find a way to work there myself. I had already spent considerable time watching the Joshua Light Show team and studying how they created their effects, and I knew that I could make a contribution with my film and photographic skills. Within days of my run-in with Jerry Pompili, I had convinced Joshua White, who headed the Joshua Light Show, to hire me — for $50 a week plus a permanent official staff pass.

I didn't have any conscious plan when I began photographing. At first, I focused on the performers who took the stage each weekend. These shots became central to my work — I even shot 16mm movie film of some acts. Soon I realized that, in both a visual and documentary sense, there was much more to the Fillmore experience than what happened onstage. Each show was the culmination of coordinated ensemble activity by dozens of people that started hours earlier and ended hours later. My role soon evolved into covering every facet of Fillmore life. My Nikons and I became so ubiquitous that Kip Cohen, the Managing Director, once compared me to a candid camera.

More than ninety people worked at the Fillmore East, and all the tasks they carried out — even the most mundane, like counting ticket stubs in the staff lounge during each show, or setting up and taking down lights and equipment — fit into the composite picture I was assembling. Almost all of us were student aged or a little older. The long hours and heady atmosphere of the counterculture vanguard caused us to bond as an extended "Fillmore family," replete with family-style relationships, tensions, jokes and rituals. The rituals included our post-concert breakfasts at Ratner's, where elderly waiters in bow ties and staid jackets would grumpily pour coffee, and dish up eggs and mushroom barley soup at 4 a.m. to an invading bunch of long-haired, bearded hippies. Often, before going to Ratner's, the crew would throw around a ball on the empty stage — this was "Noonan ball," a game invented by stagehand John Ford Noonan, who later became a noted playwright.

The backstage and dressing room scene — crowded with stars, staff and hangers-on — fascinated me, too. It was also theater! For the most part, I kept myself aloof from whatever social — or social-climbing — intrigues were going on. With my cameras in hand, in the role of observer, I steered clear of the drugs, the hype and the competing egos. But the air-kissing, hair-tossing pouting and preening certainly provided wonderful photographic fodder. Special backstage events afforded particularly striking moments. One time Bill Graham hired a Sabrett hot dog cart, complete with umbrella, to come in between two Neil Young and Crazy Horse shows and serve free hot dogs.

I loved the music at the Fillmore East, but I can say that I was IN love with the technical side of everything that went into putting on the shows, and I made it a point to take detailed photographs of all phases of these activities. The F.E. was a laboratory for experimentation in sound and music technology, and the members of the F.E. tech staff are among the unsung heroes in the development of rock performance. Many of their innovations have become industry standards. The stage hands, for example, devised a set of rolling platform risers for drum sets, so that acts and set-ups could be changed quickly. The lighting team, meanwhile, headed first by Chip Monck and later by Bruce Byall, Candace Brightman, Arthur Shafransky and George Chodorow, experimented with revolving colored gels, Super Trouper spots, dimmers and other new, dramatic ways of coordinating lighting effects with the music.

Sheer necessity forced the F.E. sound technicians to invent a whole new technology for sound reproduction. No one had resolved the problem of faithfully reproducing rock and roll's electric intonation. The mixing, microphone and speaker equipment then in use, primitive by today's standards, created serious distortions, as they were designed for different types of music — mainly classical — and stage performance.

The F.E.'s original sound system was furnished on a rental basis by "Hanley's Sound," a pioneering rock audio outfit operated by Bill Hanley.

Hanley had become successful providing sound for a number of acts, including the Jefferson Airplane. He built some custom equipment for the F.E., including mixing consoles that used professional-grade studio equipment, and he made a major contribution by insisting on top quality loud speakers. But these elements resolved only some of the problems involved in reproducing rock sound. Soon, the F.E.'s in-house tech team took over and modified Hanley's equipment, with only partial success. In the summer of 1969, the F.E. sound crew convinced Bill Graham to invest in the installation of a permanent house sound system specifically designed for rock tone and volume levels. John Chester, the F.E. Sound Engineer, aided by Technical Consultants Chris Langhart and Bob Goddard, carefully analyzed the technological causes of distortion and then designed and built revolutionary new types of multi-channel mixing boards which were among the first to use sliders instead of dials and which could automatically compensate for overload and shifting input. The F.E. sound team — John, Chris, Bob, and Steve Gagne — also designed and built a new in-house speaker system that raised the upper level of sound reproduction an octave or two. This enabled rich subtleties and overtones of performance texture to come through — the tinkle of triangles and cymbals; the full timbre of the human voice. Their goal was to create a live sound system that approached the quality of recording studio reproduction. In fact, the sound system they created was so good that the F.E. was the only venue in the world where the Grateful Dead used the in-house sound system instead of their own.

The F.E. was, from time to time, used as a recording studio. A number of live albums were recorded there, sometimes with equipment set up in the basement space under the stage and sometimes with a complete multi-track recording studio set up in a remote truck, connected to the theater by cables. Once, on a train to New York after a visit to my family in Baltimore, I was seated next to the composer Aaron Copland. He was fascinated by my stories about the F.E. operation. He told me that he had never seen rock music performed live onstage — so I brought him with me straight to the F.E. from Penn Station. The show that night featured John Mayall and Taj Mahal, and Mayall's set was being recorded for a live album, released as TURNING POINT. Copland was astonished by the technical side of the recording: He had never seen a remote recording truck. He had also never seen a light show, and the light show that evening was particularly wild. "Beautiful," Copland told me. "Just beautiful."

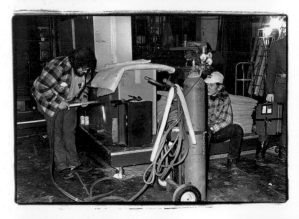  

Opposite, from top, left to right:

Kip Cohen, Managing Director of the Fillmore East.

F.E. Business Manager Jane Geraghty.

Marylou Capes, F.E. Executive Secretary from October 1970 until the closing at the end of June 1971.

Stage Manager Michael Ahern wearing one of the Fillmore East intercom headsets.

Jerry Pompili, House Manager at F.E., later VP for Bill Graham Presents.

Technical Consultant Chris Langhart. At the time he worked for Fillmore East he was a professor in charge of the Technical Theater Production Program at NYU School of the Arts.

Technical Director Bob See with a welding torch like the one he used during the performance of Tommy.

Fillmore East Sound Engineer and Designer John Chester, left, with Associate Soundman Stephen Gagne in the sound booth. The poster on the wall is the one I designed for an NYU student film production that signaled to me that the Fillmore East was where I belonged.

Soundman Lee Osborne (center), Technical Consultant Bob Goddard (right) and Hanley's Sound technician (left), in the basement under the stage. Note the mixing console and closed-circuit TV set-up.

The F.E.'s first Executive Secretary (1968 through summer 1970), Dale Franklin.

Box Office Manager Jay Benzon (left) and staff member Michael Sharp in the box office.

Josh White, left, and stagehand and playwright John Ford Noonan.

Amalie caught in the upstairs mezzanine lobby with her camera gear, December 31, 1969.

The marquee in December 1969.

The front left showcase and the R.D. Laing quotation banner which hung over the Fillmore East entrance for several weeks between the end of December 1969 and the beginning of January 1970.

The main entrance doors where tickets were collected seen from the inner lobby.

Patrons in line at the box office in the outer lobby.

Jay Benzon sells tickets to the last show, June 1971. Note the box-office graffiti.

A rare interior view of the theater taken from the orchestra section facing the sound booth. Clearly visible are the slightly worn and chipped bas relief painted plaster decorations, columns and other ornamentation from the theater's earlier days as a vaudeville, Yiddish Theater and movie house. The doorway with the "Exit" sign was the entrance to the backstage area. The box on the other side of the stage, behind where I'm standing, was the lighting control booth. In the picture you can also see some of the permanently installed lighting equipment, including one of the follow spot positions, with operator, above the sound booth box between the capitals of the two columns flanking the booth.

The balcony at Fillmore East.

Welcome to the Fillmore East, 1969. This is the view patrons saw as they entered the hall to be seated by ushers before a show.

The Grateful Dead at Fillmore East, January 2, 1970. I consider this my definitive F.E. concert shot. It was rare that I could get all the members of a band clearly visible with uniform lighting, and even rarer to be able to include and see the audience as well.

Paul Butterfield Blues Band with Joe's Lights background, March 21, 1971.

Opposite:

The Joshua Light Show holiday group portrait, December 1969. From left to right: Gene Thiel, Amalie R. Rothschild, Ken Richman, Tom Shoesmith, Jane Rixman, Bill Schwarzbach, Joshua White, Cecily Hoyt.

THEATER OF LIGHT: THE JOSHUA LIGHT SHOW

"An electric guitar wails though a haze of screaming feedback; a visceral bass pushes forward the beat; drums punch wild with pure, throbbing emotion; and a singer writhes sweating at the mike. Above and behind, the music is mirrored in color: great swirling shapes shimmer and blend, give birth and die. Strobes pepper the air with bursts of flame. Visuals swoop and flutter, too fast for awareness. Sound and image come alive: they dazzle, they embrace; they explode; they are one......"

In overheated retrospect, nothing in visual terms defined psychedelia like the light shows of the 1960s. The sensual, dancing colors and flashing bursts of light meshed perfectly with freeform, electric rock in an intense incarnation of the counterculture revolution — not to mention the mind-blowing hallucinogenic experience brought on by acid, mescaline, grass and all the other drugs that circulated so freely.

The heyday of the light shows lasted only a few short years, but their influence is still palpable. Whether simple, amateur efforts or complicated technical tours de force, they pioneered the multimedia combination of sound and image that eventually became a staple on MTV and other outlets; they were, indeed, the precursors of today's music videos and their influence can still be felt in popular culture. Rock groups today often use spectacular light shows as part of their concerts, but from the technological and conceptual points of view they are quite different from the pioneering light shows that played venues such as the F.E. The big difference is that the light shows of the '60S were live performances in their own right, not push-button products of computer programming and video projection. The people behind the scenes who manipulated film, overhead and slide projectors, color organs, strobe lights and a wealth of other equipment were just as much performers as the musicians onstage. In a sense they were puppeteers —

but their puppets were fleeting intangibles projected on a screen.

The Joshua Light Show, named after its director, Joshua White, was arguably the best in the business and fully deserved the special separate billing it got under the Fillmore East marquee. At the F.E., the light show was never used as visual background noise, an abstract extravaganza to entertain the crowd between sets. Each show, each night, was a complex theatrical production: an intricate collage of colors and images that melded with the music and took half a dozen or more artists to perform.

The seeds for the Joshua Light Show were sown amid the bland wholesomeness of the 1950s. "It was a drab time," Josh once reminisced, "then the '60s came along and anything that lit up or strobed or flashed or turned from red to amber was what everybody was looking for." Josh, Bill Schwarzbach, and Tom Shoesmith had all been "techies" at Carnegie Tech University in Pittsburgh or at Columbia University in New York. All three simply loved light and loved what creative use of technology could do with it. After college they started doing lighting at discos and fashion shows and then branched out. They first staged a full-scale light show for Bill Graham at a concert Graham promoted in Toronto in 1967. He loved it. When the

Fillmore East opened its doors a few months later, in March 1968, Graham hired the team — by now known as the Joshua Light Show — and gave them headline billing along with the changing roster of bands. By the time I joined the Joshua Light Show in April 1969, its working members included Cecily Hoyt, Ken Richman and Jane Rixman, in addition to Josh, Bill and Tom. When Josh left the show in 1970, the number of personnel was expanded and the name of the ensemble was changed to Joe's Lights.

At the Fillmore East, the light show employed a complex battery of equipment, most of it designed and specially built in-house, and none of it ever seen by the audience. Every effect was produced by rear projection. The equipment was permanently set up backstage on a two-tiered platform attached to the rear brick wall of the theater and aimed at the back of a huge screen about twenty feet away. All the imagery was projected onto this screen, which formed the backdrop to the stage itself. The audience saw the images coming through it on the other side.

The light show repertoire involved several closely coordinated elements that fell into the two broad categories of "wet show" and "dry show."

The "wet show," the pulsating, abstract shapes of color that were produced by as many as three overhead projectors, was the most easily recognizable — by now a cliché hallmark of the psychedelic era. The projected images that bubbled across the screen like giant amoebas were created with a combination of colored glycerins, alcohols, oils and water, laid out on curved clear glass plates. Cecily Hoyt was brilliant with the overhead projectors and moving liquid effects, and she was also responsible for creating all the liquids and dyes. Each batch of colored oil had to be prepared with meticulous care — a speck of dust or stray hair or other impurity would show up onscreen, magnified a thousand times. It also took tremendous control to get the various blobs of color to pulsate in just the right way at just the right time and to move in sync with the music.

For projection plates, the show used the convex glass fronts of commercially manufactured clocks, choosing various sizes for various effects. A larger sized plate on the bottom carried a water base on which the carefully dribbled blobs of colored oil floated. A smaller clock face was then pressed carefully atop this, squishing the oils into patterns. Moving and jiggling this upper plate produced the sensuous pulsations of the projected images.

Other marbleized images were produced by dribbling streaks of color onto a projection base and then blowing them into patterns with a hairdryer. It was all delicate but incredibly messy work — an essential piece of equipment was a dishwasher right on the light show platform.

The only lights powerful enough to produce projected images that were strong and bright enough onscreen were airport landing lights. They got so hot that the oil and water in the plates would eventually start to boil. This potential problem, however, produced one of the light show's signature effects — the "boiling plate," where the colors literally bubbled and boiled away onscreen. Bill Schwarzbach was the technical visionary who devised the custom-built overhead projectors and found the airport landing lights. He also had the creativity to transform seeming disasters like the boiling plate into effects that became important hallmarks of the light show.

The "dry show" — a wide variety of slides, 16mm film, film strips and loops, and other projectables — supplemented the "wet show" by building up layers of still and moving images that interacted with the pulsating colors. At the F.E., the light show used two banks of four carousel slide projectors, so the slides could be used both for single images — including flashing messages, individual words or the names of the groups onscreen — and also for repetitive, multiple patterns. These effects could be further enhanced by projecting the slides through variegated color wheels that were controlled by rheostats to revolve at different speeds. Light and projected images were also bounced off rotating, handmade mirror wheels painstakingly constructed by piecing together mosaic-like shards of broken mirrors.

I provided many of the graphic images for the slide archive and also shot and edited the bulk of the 16mm film material, both loops and running footage. Some of this material was aimed at producing a purely abstract effect — such as the endlessly non-repeating wave forms I shot off an oscilloscope, the abstract effect of the girders of the 59th Street Bridge, or the flashing tracks of lights I shot in the Queens Midtown Tunnel, or the striking, high contrast geometric patterns I created on slides. But I also shot narrative footage for special productions. The show used three movie projectors — one fixed, wide-angle projector, plus one on which material was run "straight," and one small hand-held projector, which was used with loops to produce moving effects that ranged across the screen. In addition to pure light, graphic images and footage, the show projected cartoons (two

The Allman Brothers Band with a Joe's Lights background at the last concert at Fillmore East, June 27, 1971.

Dennis Clark and Cecily Hoyt, with Allan Arkush looking on, demo-ing wet plates on the overhead projectors.

Tom Shoesmith demonstrating his Lumia equipment on the upper platform. Note the white bird reflected on the Mylar sheet he's holding.

favorites were "The Sunshine Makers" and "Flat Flip Flies Straight") and other material between sets, as well as the names of the groups, announcements, odd sayings and other word play and verbal imagery.

Adding to these "wet" and "dry" effects, most of which were projected from the lower platform, Tom Shoesmith worked autonomously on the upper level. He was a Lumia artist: his specialty was the exploitation of every kind of material that could reflect light. He employed a small battery of projectors with intense light sources. Typically, he used them to throw images onto a flexible, hand-held Mylar mirror sheet, which he then manipulated manually to reflect the images, now distorted, and re-project them back onto the light show screen in moving patterns.

The light shows were a mix of improvisation and control. The effects were created by individual members of the team, but everything was coordinated by a master "mixer" who acted like an orchestra conductor and controlled what was actually shown onscreen, in what combination, and for how long. This, for the Joshua Light Show, was usually Joshua White. "Every week we had new ideas, which

became part of a whole palette of ideas, and it was my job to mix those ideas together," he has recalled. "Each person focussed on his or her area, and I focussed on the show. I was the only one who focussed on the show as a whole. It was my job to be, in essence, the conductor. The real performance, the real art, was being done by the soloists — Bill and Cecily on the overheads; Tom on the Lumia. I was mixing the show and adding lots of details."

Josh said he realized very quickly that the Light Show's trademark style was going to be the use of abstraction. "All the other sophisticated light shows had a tendency to be slide oriented," he said. "If a band was singing a song about a chair, they'd project a collage of chairs. Our light show, though, was 98 percent abstraction. So that if they sang a song about a chair, there would be a thirty- and later a forty-foot wide screen with amazing movement on it, and in the middle would be a chair, which I would place there, and the audience would make the right connections. It was fun — like taking a silent movie and putting music to it. Everything gets into sync, and you sync it in your mind — and the audience did that visually with the light show. They synched what they saw on the

From left to right: Allan Arkush, Ken Richman, Bill Schwarzbach demonstrating some of the many projectors used by the light show.

Ken Richman at the mixing console showing all the various dimmers and other projector controls.

Cecily Hoyt demonstrates a wet plate on the overhead projector. Note the mirror wheel at left of frame.

The light show's liquid oil and glycerin bottles. Each one is a different color and/or viscosity.

Cecily Hoyt preparing dyes for the light show wet media.

Becky Smith prepping some of the light show wet plates for the dishwasher on the platform during a show.

The light show slide table on the light show platform

screen to what they were feeling, and, especially when people tended to take a lot of drugs, the very abstraction of the light show gave each person a personal experience."

Josh and the other mixers, including Ken Richman and later, after the show became Joe's Lights, Allan Arkush, worked from an adapted lighting control board. Every light, every projector, was hooked up to it, enabling the effects to be faded in or faded out as desired. Whoever worked a show as mixer was in constant communication with the others in the team via intercom headsets, and everyone would discuss and agree on upcoming imagery, based on the music being played. The mixer would then orchestrate the visual performance. The effects were very theatrical. "In fact, our goal became seeing how many things we could do," Josh said. "Since we came from a theater background, we understood the discipline of changing when the music changed, moving when the music moved, standing still when the music stood still."

It was intensive, exacting, grueling work, as the light show performed with almost every act that appeared onstage. That meant as many as six sets, backing three different groups, in one long night. But the effort and energy produced memorable effects. "As each new tech-

nical element came along, we exploited it," Josh has recalled. "For example, we had one set of strips with various buttons hooked up to lights. Push that button, and the screen turned red. Push another button and the red lights went off and yellow lights went on. Press another button and the yellow lights went off and the green lights went on. We were able to go red, yellow, green so fast that the people saw white. But the kind of white they saw was not 'pure' white, but white made up of many colors — and that's something really stunning. We ended up with a range of expression where we could go from something as quick and pithy as a strobe, where at the press of a button the screen would be white for a nanosecond, to something as slow and as graceful as one of Tom's evolving Lumia effects, or one of Bill's slow pouring of liquid over the top of the projector — he was doing things chemically that literally sometimes took half an hour to evolve; things involving convection currents from the projector which would carry color upward and then out to the edge where it would sink and come back toward the center and rise again — onscreen you would see stuff coming at you and have no idea at all how it was done."

All this was possible because of the Light Show's permanent set-up at the Fillmore East, and above all because

of the extraordinary communication system that linked the light show personnel, the stage and lighting crew, and other members of the technical team. This system was one of the early innovations at the Fillmore East. Everything was on closed-circuit television and everyone was connected via a headset intercom system. The light show people were thus in constant contact with the stage crew and everyone else and could follow the stage show on TV monitors. The headset chatter was often hilarious; in addition to passing on cues and commands, staff members were unsparing in their critiques of onstage acts and offstage egos. The communication system was designed and custom-built by John Chester, the F.E. Audio Engineer – who went on to perfect and install such systems in other venues. John holds several patents on this intercom technology and it has become an industry standard for TV, multi-media and rock and roll touring operations.

I found photographing the light shows an enormous challenge. The curved light show screen spanned the whole stage, and the swirling colors and images seemed to leap out and enfold the entire theater. Given the limitations and light sensitivity of the fastest color 35mm film of the time, High Speed Ektachrome 160 ASA, even pushed two stops there was no real way of capturing this all-embracing effect. In the photographs, thus, the light show images seem oddly concentrated at one central point of the screen, emerging like vignettes from darker, shadowy margins that frame the shots.

Still, I think the images capture some of the immediacy of an experience that even the best of today's hi-tech light shows cannot quite match. At the Fillmore East, the light show was a hands-on creative effort; each separate effect was produced by an individual artist working together with other artists. Light show technology has evolved dramatically since then, enabling spectacular effects at the touch of a button or computer key and multiple images built up from video projections. However, exciting as many contemporary light shows are, they strike me as remote and somehow unsatisfying in their clean, choreographed perfection — like polished and edited recordings, perhaps, rather than living, breathing, rock theater.

Joshua Light Show and Joe's Lights images. The upper strip shows Virgil Fox at Fillmore East, December 1, 1970. The lower strip shows an evolving Lumia sequence performed by Tom Shoesmith.

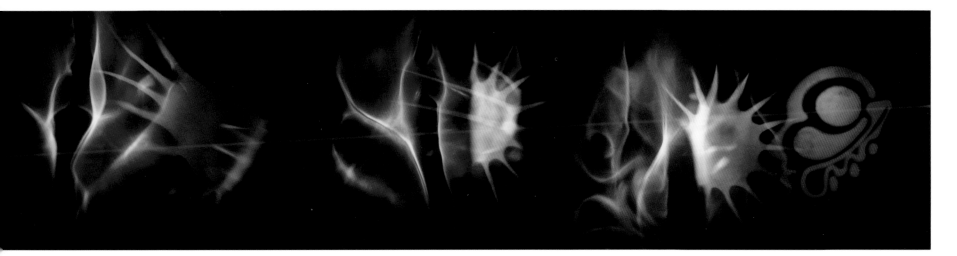

The bedlam backstage during the Joshua Light Show's second birthday party, December 1969. You can see how people were hamming it up for me while I took this picture. At left Josh White can be seen groping Kip Cohen's wife Lynn, while Kip looks on smiling. Josh and Kip went to college together and were old buddies. Kip and Lynn are still a happy couple. Meanwhile, further to the right in the photo "Boots," a sometime light show roadie, points out the scene. At the right lower corner is the cake being cut by Keeva Kristal, Bill Graham's old friend from his days waiting tables in the Catskills, who filled in for Kip from time to time as Fillmore East Acting Managing Director.

The Joshua Light Show with their four tons of equipment on their two platforms suspended from the back wall at Fillmore East.
From left to right: Jane Rixmann, Cecily Hoyt, Bill Schwarzbach, Tom Shoesmith (upper platform), Josh White, Ken Richman.
It was quite an ordeal to remove and store all of this equipment on the infrequent occasions when other light shows performed,
most notably Glenn McKay's Headlights which travelled with the Jefferson Airplane, and the Pig Light Show.

A selection of images from the Joshua Light Show and Joe's Lights.

Full house at the Fillmore East, date unknown. This picture was taken from the follow spot booth which used to house the movie projectors when it was the Loew's Commodore theater.

LADIES AND GENTLEMEN, LIVE ON STAGE...

During its short lifetime, the legendary stage of Bill Graham's transformed old movie house was THE New York rock venue, the undisputed East Coast Mecca for the music that formed the soundtrack of the '60s. But rock wasn't the only type of music played at the F.E.

Graham always tried to challenge the audience, to expose them to something new — and above all to something good. The F.E. featured four main shows a week — two on Friday night and two on Saturday, with the early show starting at 8 p.m., and the late one starting around 11:30 and running sometimes until 3 a.m. or later. Each show usually featured three groups, and Graham sought deliberately to mix and match different musical genres and styles. He wanted to open minds as well as ears, so he would book a down-home blues singer, for example, or a jazz great like Buddy Guy who was little known to psychedelic rock fans, as an opening act for popular headliners such as Jefferson Airplane or The Who. Or he would book gospel, blues or acoustic acts side by side with heavy electric bands. With this creative programming approach, as one reviewer at the time put it, Graham was acting like a connoisseur at a wine tasting who carefully sampled a piece of good cheese to clear his palate between two fine vintages.

Still, I was surprised one afternoon to hear someone practicing Robert Schumann's Piano Concerto in A on the F.E. piano. I was working up on the light show platform sorting out new slide material before a show, and I could hardly believe my ears. That concerto is one of my favorite pieces of classical music, and whoever was playing it was really good. I climbed down to investigate; the pianist turned out to be Keith Emerson, at that time with the Nice, who, I then discovered, was a classically trained musician.

Graham used the Fillmore stage, too, to introduce new groups and performers: for almost six months, Tuesday nights were devoted to introducing little known, often local, groups for a flat $1.50 admission. He refused, though, he once told an interviewer, to pad his shows with what he called "mashed potatoes" — cheap support acts that fans would grit their teeth and endure in order to hear a big name artist. In many ways, Graham said, he modeled the F.E. on the famed Apollo Theater in Harlem: If a performer was good and had something to say, he would know, as Graham put it, that the F.E. was where he could just go out onstage and do it. Success at the Fillmore East could bring instant fame and lead to concert tours and record contracts, and the F.E. became the American launching pad for a number of English acts in particular — Jethro Tull, Ten Years After, Fleetwood Mac, and Joe Cocker and the Grease Band, among others.

In photographing the performers, my main concern was with the aesthetics of the pictures I was taking. But I was also strongly influenced by the music. I rarely photographed bands whose music I didn't like — after all, I wasn't being paid to photograph anyone in particular, so I was free to pick and choose my subjects. I think this attitude comes out clearly in my pictures. I shot roll after roll of performers I enjoyed — like Janis Joplin, or Jimi Hendrix, or B.B. King — and the pictures themselves reflect my appreciation of their music. I also followed the stars backstage, capturing casual moments between sets and before and after performances. It amazed me, sometimes, how people who looked so crazy and acted so larger-than-life in front of an audience would shrink back into human dimensions when out of the spotlight.

I was rarely satisfied with just shooting single frames, particularly of acts onstage. This went back to my experience in film — I never thought just one single frame could tell the whole story. So I often shot sequential images, and sometimes, too, I carefully composed multiple exposure images in the camera. Today, computers and digital imaging technology can easily create such multiple compositions, but at the time, it was a real artistic and technical challenge to achieve that effect directly on film.

I began taking occasional pictures of rock performers in early 1968, around the time the F.E. opened — I photographed Jimi Hendrix at the Cafe Au Go Go in March of that year, for example. But Joni Mitchell is the first performer I actually remember photographing at the Fillmore East. It was April 25, 1969. I had gone along to the early show without my cameras, just to hear the music. Joni wore a beautiful red velvet dress that night, and I was so struck by the way she looked, the way she moved, her expressions, her graceful way of physically relating to what she was singing and playing — in a visual as well as aural sense — that I ran home and grabbed my cameras and came back to the second show, just to photograph her.

Joni was the headline act that night on a bill that also included James Cotton and Taj Mahal — and Taj Mahal became one of my favorite acts to shoot, both onstage and behind the scenes. Taj was one of the few performers I got to know personally. He could discuss the folk

Jerry Garcia at the Fillmore East, September 27, 1969.

roots of the music he was playing within an intellectual and historical framework; he could express verbally the emotional creative process of translating folk motifs into his own musical art. Onstage, I loved the way the colorful, African-influenced clothing he often wore made a perfect foil for the light show projections behind him, and I played with these combinations in my photographs. Crosby, Stills, Nash & Young, on the other hand, presented other exciting, but totally different, visual possibilities. The group was one of the few acts whose F.E. performances were not accompanied by a light show. They felt a light show background would be distracting. Instead, the group sang elegantly spotlit in front of a deep black background, perched on stools atop a plush Persian carpet laid across the stage.

Janis Joplin played the Fillmore East a number of times, both with Big Brother and as a headliner in her own right, and I have numerous pictures of her. She was an incredibly physical performer, throwing herself into the music. She didn't politely "perspire" when she performed — she sweated, and sweated hard. She didn't "make love" to her audience — she ripped out a piece of her heart and had raw, visceral sex with them. She was mesmerizing. Like the rest of the audience, I would absolutely lose myself in her performance. This series of pictures is from a concert she gave on February 11, 1969 — I took frame after frame of her at this show, but I was so wrapped up in the performance itself that I don't remember taking them at all.

Jimi Hendrix was a perfect subject to photograph. Onstage, he was one of the most charismatic, and most sensual, performers ever. The way he moved, the way he played, the way he caressed the music, the guitar, the lyrics, even the way he dressed, exuded sexuality. But offstage he was quite different — I found him natural, unaffected, even shy. The pictures I took of Hendrix relaxing backstage show this side of him — particularly the photo of him with two of the young members of the Voices of East Harlem, taken at New Years, 1969/1970.

The New Year's Eve and New Year's Day concerts that Hendrix and his new group Band of Gypsys, with the Voices of East Harlem as opening act, played December 31, 1969 and January 1, 1970, were among the most memorable events of the Fillmore East years. For one thing, they marked the (chronological, at least) end of the '60s. Also, they were the debut shows by Hendrix's new, all black, band. A lot of preparation went into the New Year's Eve concert in particular to make it a really special experience. This meant touches like placing a tambourine on every seat so that the audience could take part in the occasion, to concocting special light show effects and

Country Joe McDonald at Fillmore East, September 27, 1969.

The Nice with Keith Emerson at Fillmore East, December 20, 1969.

Quicksilver Messenger Service at Fillmore East, April 4, 1970.

Joni Mitchell at Fillmore East, April 25, 1969. This is a triple exposure shot in the camera.

Jimi Hendrix at Cafe Au Go Go, March 17, 1968. This is one of my first rock music pictures.

New York Mayor John Lindsay during the "Springtime for Lowenstein" benefit, March 21, 1971. The benefit was held to raise funds to cover campaign debts for New York liberal Democratic Congressman Allard Lowenstein who was murdered several years later.

Satirical singer Tom Lehrer performing at the "Springtime for Lowenstein" benefit.

New York Congresswoman Bella Abzug at the "Springtime for Lowenstein" benefit.

Comedian David Steinberg during the "Springtime for Lowenstein" benefit.

material. For example, I shot an opening sequence in 16mm for the Joshua Light Show to program with the Voices of East Harlem's set. I filmed the young singers leaving their homes in Harlem, getting on the subway to go downtown, exiting at 8th Street, pushing the cube sculpture at Astor Place and then running down Second Avenue past Ratner's, under the F.E. marquee and into the theater. This sequence was projected onto the light show screen that embraced the Fillmore stage as an introduction to the act. As the singers were seen running into the theater onscreen, they came running down the aisles from the back of the hall and jumped onstage and launched into their first number. Then, as midnight approached, we flashed a huge countdown onscreen — 10, 9, 8, 7, 6 — with everybody shouting out the numbers together, getting higher and higher, louder and louder. As the clock struck midnight we raised the light show screen to reveal staff, crew and musicians all together onstage — including Jimi Hendrix, who threw himself into an extraordinary rendition of Auld Lang Syne that rivaled the signature rendition of the Star Spangled Banner he had played at Woodstock a few months earlier.

The Grateful Dead were almost a house band at the Fillmore East — they played there twenty-seven times. They were really the favorite band of the entire F.E. staff. Of course, the Dead were part of the San Francisco scene that had coalesced around the original Fillmore Auditorium and Fillmore West, so they were really sort of family. The Dead would play long, long intricate sets, and they'd stay onstage as long as they felt like it — until 3 or 4 in the morning — or as long as the audience wanted them to stay. They'd play encore after encore; people just didn't want them to leave, and they were happy to keep on playing. Already the Dead were attaining that cult status where fans would follow them from gig to gig and camp out on the sidewalk overnight in order to get tickets. In fact, the first time people camped out for tickets at the F.E. was for a Dead concert, and it was such a surprise that I took pictures of them lining the pavement in their sleeping bags.

For us working at the Fillmore East, concerts by the Dead could prove a challenge in a different way — members of the Dead and their entourage used to try to dose people with LSD. It was a cardinal rule never to drink out of an open can or a cup when the Dead were playing unless we wanted to risk an unexpected acid trip. We even knew to wipe off the moisture from an UNopened can before drinking, just in case that was spiked, too. The first time I tripped out was when Owlsley, the notorious acid producer and the Dead's soundman at the time, slipped acid into my drink when we were up in the sound booth together. I never had wanted to try acid, but when I realized what was happening I didn't panic at all; the trip became a positive experience: joyous, happy and liberating.

One night the Dead managed to dose Bill Graham with acid. Getting Bill high had been a big challenge for them — he was not into drugs at all, partly out of a sense that he had to stay in control on the job in the midst of all the crazy psychedelic stuff going on around him. I photographed Graham standing behind a speaker column onstage, partly hidden from the audience, stoned out of his mind, playing his favorite instrument, a cowbell.

When Graham was at the F.E., he often hung out onstage during performances — usually behind that speaker column at stage left. He liked the music of most of the acts he booked, but you could tell who his favorites were when you saw him lurking in the wings. Another picture shows him crouching in the shadows during a February 17, 1971 performance by Rod Stewart and Ron Wood.

What I particularly liked about the Dead in a professional sense was that they and their music were a catalyst for rock theater. Sometimes, for example, Dead shows were emceed by a bizarre, zombie-like character named Zacherle, a WNEW disk jockey who also gained fame as the host of late-night TV horror movies. And their performance and personal style as a whole included theatrical touches that gave those of us working the light show tremendous scope for inventive presentation. Two examples stand out.

One was the setup of a mirror ball for the song "Dark Star." Today, the concept of sparkling lights shooting off a mirror ball is outright retro — if not an obligatory feature of every fly-by-night disco or tacky cocktail lounge. But what the F.E. tech crew set up with the Dead was a truly creative concept at the time. Everyone backstage was cued in as to when "Dark Star" was going to be played during the set. Suddenly, without explanation, the lights went out in the entire house, leaving the audience sitting in complete darkness, totally black. It was like suddenly going blind. Then the band began to play, with that very slow guitar rhythm that starts the song. The music started to build mysteriously there in the dark; the tension mounted. When the sense of anticipation became almost unbearable, Bam! The music broke out. At that exact moment pure white spotlights hit a huge spinning mirror ball, which had been lowered over the audience, sending millions of stars shooting out all over the hall. I remember hearing — and feeling — a collective gasp from the audience the first time we did this. I caught my breath, too, even though I knew what was about to happen. It was a remarkable group experience, as if we had all been suddenly transported into the middle of the universe with all the stars flying around, filling the air.

Welding and constructing the new curved light show screen for Tommy, *October 1969.*

Gail Rodgers and friend preparing the flower vases for the dressing rooms on a Friday afternoon. Bill Graham had a deal with the local florist. In exchange for a free ad in the weekly Fillmore East program the florist would supply the theater with all his unsold flowers at the end of the week.

From left to right: Lee Erdman, George Merriman, Michael Klenfner, Tony Mazzucchi et al moving in the rented Super Trouper lighting equipment for the New Year's show, December 31, 1969.

From left to right: Assistant Technical Director Tony Mazzucchi, Stu Hutter and stage-hand loading a group's equipment into the theater on a Friday afternoon.

Delaney & Bonnie Bramlett and friends with Eric Clapton at Fillmore East, February 7, 1970.

Opposite:
Laura Nyro at Fillmore East, June 20, 1970.

The other stand-out theatrical experience with the Dead involved the film projections and show we organized for their trademark song "Casey Jones," which they frequently used to open their set. My friend David Vartanoff, who processed much of my color film, was a train buff. He was crazy about the old steam locomotives that used to be brought out to make a run once a year between Hoboken, New Jersey, and Binghamton, New York. He wanted to chase a train, and we decided to film it to get footage for a light show presentation for "Casey Jones." We chased the train for a whole weekend and managed to intercept and film it about a dozen times. I got great footage that ended up being used over and over again as part of the light show. The best shot came from one particular place where the train came around a long curve. I had brought a giant Angenieux 25 to 250mm zoom lens with me and set up the camera so that it was aligned with the curve — I was able to use the zoom so that the huge old engine, belching smoke, slowly came right up into the frame, rounded the curve and then went whooshing by as I drew the lens back, catching a dramatic shot of the entire locomotive, all incredible speed and power, roaring down the track. It was very effective, and we used that piece of footage for the opening of many Dead shows. We also used it for the opening of the Allman Brothers last set at the very last concert at the F.E. on June 27, 1971.

Joe Cocker with Mad Dogs & Englishmen at Fillmore East, March 28, 1970. There must have been at least fifty people in the Cocker entourage onstage for this series of shows, more than at any other time during the F.E., perhaps because the Mad Dogs tour was being filmed for a movie. You can see two cameramen in this photo, one at the extreme left of the frame and the other crouching at right. Also, look carefully and you can see that Cocker is wearing only socks on his feet. He had given his fancy shoes to a patron in the first row and you can see the white shoes with stars on them propped up on the front of the stage at the bottom edge of the picture.

Joe Cocker with Mad Dogs and Englishmen, March 28, 1970.

Janis Joplin at Fillmore East, February 11, 1969.

John Fogerty of Creedence Clearwater Revival at Fillmore East with Joshua Light Show background, March 22, 1969.

Ken Richman of the Joshua Light Show demonstrating an array of equipment including slide projectors with color wheels and the title overhead projector.

Opposite:

Top left: Dizzy Gillespie at Fillmore East, April 18, 1970.

Top right: Lesley West of Mountain at Fillmore East, June 27, 1971.

Bottom: Chuck Berry at Fillmore East, October 3, 1969.

Taj Mahal at Fillmore East, February 11, 1971.

Taj Mahal and the four tubas against a Joe's Lights background, February 11, 1971. This weekend was probably the best series of concerts Taj gave at Fillmore East and this is my favorite black & white light show photograph.

A view of the house from the balcony during the Band of Gypsys sound check, December 31, 1969.

Jimi Hendrix and Band of Gypsys sound check, Fillmore East, December 31, 1969.

Jimi Hendrix backstage with two of the Voices of East Harlem, December 31, 1969.

The tambourines on each seat given to concert go-ers to celebrate the New Year's Eve Jimi Hendrix and Band of Gypsys show, December 31, 1969.

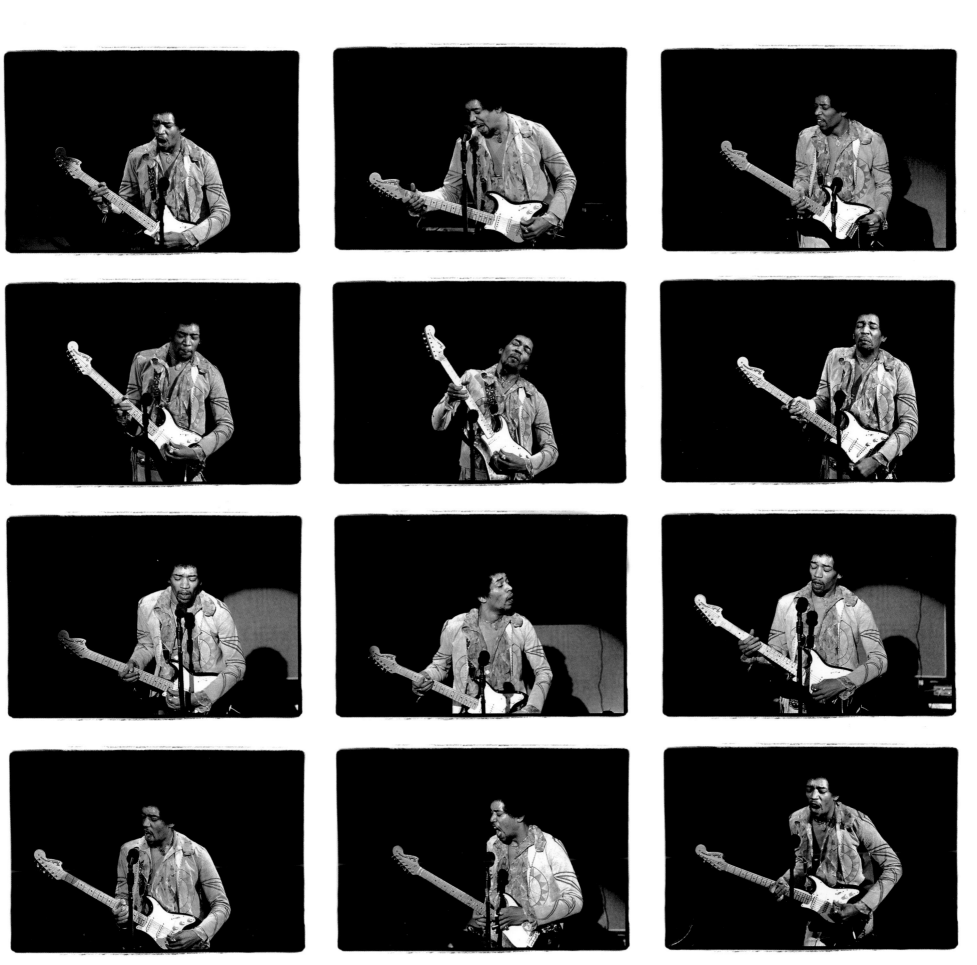

Jimi Hendrix at Fillmore East, December 31, 1969.

The Voices of East Harlem at Fillmore
East, August 12, 1970

"Happy Fillmore New Year" T-shirts
being worn by stage crew. Backstage
scene, December 31, 1969.

An ushers' and house staff meeting in the inner lobby prior to a concert. Most people are sitting on the steps up to the mezzanine and balcony.

Ushers lolling about before opening the house for a Friday evening early show.

Ushers and house security staff during a pre-show crew meeting.

Tina Turner and the Ikettes perform at Fillmore East, January 10, 1970.

Tina Turner and the Ikettes at F.E., January 9, 1970.

Van Morrison performing at the NET taping on September 23, 1970.

Eric Clapton at Fillmore East,
February 6, 1970.

The audience at Fillmore East during the taping of the first rock music TV show by National Educational Television (NET), September 23, 1970. The extra lights installed for the TV cameras made photographing this concert much easier than usual. In particular, they allowed me to get pictures of the audience which I could rarely get under normal conditions since it was usually shrouded in darkness.

Top:
Terry Reid at Fillmore East, July 18, 1969.

Bottom:
Felix Pappalardi and Lesley West of Mountain at the Fillmore East's last concert, June 27, 1971.

Top:
Van Morrison at Fillmore East, April 3, 1970.

Bottom:
Nina Simone at Fillmore East, May 30, 1970.

The audience during the NET show taping, September 23, 1970.

Sha Na Na performing "Teen Angel" during the NET videotaping at Fillmore East, September 23, 1970.

Janis Joplin at Fillmore East, February 12, 1969.

Ray Charles at Fillmore East, April 18, 1970.

Carlos Santana at Fillmore East, April 3, 1971.

Roberta Flack at Fillmore East, February 11, 1971.

Carlos Santana at Fillmore East, April 3, 1971

Elton John at Fillmore East, April 8, 1971.

Fillmore East patrons

Barry Melton of Country Joe and the Fish writhing onstage, September 27, 1969.

Crosby, Stills and Nash at F.E., June 3, 1970.

Neil Young with Manager Eliott Roberts (center) and Leo Makota (right) in dressing room at Fillmore East, March 6, 1970.

Neil Young and Crazy Horse sound check, March 6, 1970.

A view of the stage from the sound booth during a Leon Russell concert, May 22, 1971. This is the view special guests saw since the sound booth was used for VIP seating. I shot many pictures from this position.

Backstage scene with John Cipolina of Quicksilver Messenger Service's guitar being carried onstage, April 4, 1970.

Backstage party, March 6, 1970. Between the early and late shows during the Neil Young and Crazy Horse concerts Bill Graham hired a Sabrett hot dog vendor to feed everyone.

A backstage crowd scene at Fillmore East, May 8, 1970. Bill Graham with Mike Klenfner, left, and Steve Rosenfeld, right, Recording Engineer Eddie Kramer standing in black jacket, Frank Zappa in lower right corner.

Frank Zappa backstage at Fillmore East, May 8, 1970. I took the picture from the hallway of the first level dressing rooms.

Frank Zappa backstage at Fillmore East, May 8, 1970. For this angle, I stood on the steps to the 2nd level dressing rooms. Zappa is sitting in the doorway entrance to the light show platform.

Backstage boogie-ing. Note the short distance between the light show platform at right and the rear of the light show screen at left of frame.

Light show screen emergency. During a performance a rope gave way and the screen fell, date not remembered. It was repaired quickly and the show resumed after a short intermission. Crew from left to right: Billy Chesboro, Arthur Shafransky, Alex Masabki, Peter Sundelin, Ben Haller, (above) Doug Rye, George Chodorow, Bob See, John Chester, (standing onstage) Michael Ahern.

The new Fillmore East sound system designed by John Chester (on ladder), Chris Langhart and Bob Goddard, just before it was hoisted into position, late summer 1969.

A scene backstage, February 11, 1971. I have talked with both Stage Manager Michael Ahern (third from left in photo) and Security Chief Mike Klenfner (to his right), and neither of them remember who the nude young woman was or why she was sitting there. I can't remember either.

Backstage after a Grateful Dead concert, January 2, 1970.

Camping out for Grateful Dead tickets, May 1970.

Camping out for Grateful Dead tickets, May 1970. This was the first time at Fillmore East that a crowd of young people gathered overnight to hold their places in line. Soon this became a common sight.

The Grateful Dead, the Allman Brothers and Mick Fleetwood jamming at Fillmore East, February 11, 1970. The Deadhead underground audio tape of this performance is legendary. I can credit John Dwork, who publishes "Dupree's Diamond News," a Deadhead fanzine, with recognizing the content of this picture and dating it for me. From what he tells me, it's the only known photograph of this historic moment.

Jerry Garcia and Bob Weir backstage, February 11, 1970.

Bill Graham, tripping on LSD, plays his cowbell half hidden by a speaker column onstage at Fillmore East with the Grateful Dead, sometime in 1969.

The Grateful Dead at Fillmore East, February 14, 1970.

Some members of the Grateful Dead backstage at Fillmore East, February 11, 1970. From left to right: Pigpen Ron McKernan, Manager Jon McIntire, Jerry Garcia, Bob Weir.

Taj Mahal in dressing room with Howard Johnson and another band member, February 11, 1971.

Jerry Garcia backstage during one of his rare clean-shaven periods, May 15, 1970.

The Grateful Dead's infamous soundman and LSD chemist, Owlsley, a.k.a. Bear, Fillmore East, February 11, 1970.

Stephen Stills' guitar cases in dressing room, June 3, 1970.

Robin Williamson and girlfriend Licorice MacKechnie of the group Incredible String Band backstage in a dressing room at Fillmore East, April 25, 1970.

Opposite: *from top, left to right:*

The box-office concert board.

Jack Casady and Marty Balin of Jefferson Airplane, backstage.

Fillmore East stage crew: from left to right, Tony Mazzucchi (kneeling), Mark Kruger, Tom Mohler, Dan Opatoshu, Michael Ahern, George Chodorow (kneeling).

Joe Glackin, Marty Balin, Bill Graham, and Chris Kelly backstage.

Bill Graham and Kip Cohen with Jorma Kaukonen of Jefferson Airplane backstage.

Anti-War posters in the Fillmore East lobby, winter 1969-70.

TICKETS NOW ON SALE

MARCH 6-7 *SOLD OUT* NEIL YOUNG and Crazy Horse STEVE MILLER BLUES BAND EXTRA ADDED ATTRACTION: MILES DAVIS QUINTET

MARCH 13-14 *SOLD OUT* JOHN MAYALL w/ Dexter Bennett B.B. KING TAJ MAHAL

SUNDAY MARCH 15 8:30 PM JOHN MAYALL w/ Dexter Bennett TAJ MAHAL

THURSDAY, MARCH 19 8:30 PM MOODY BLUES LEE MICHAELS ARGENT

ON SALE MARCH 11

TUES. & WED. APRIL 28-29 JEFFERSON AIRPLANE MANFRED MANN CHAPTER THREE Glenn McKay's HEAD LIGHTS

MARCH 20-21 *SOLD OUT* MOODY BLUES LEE MICHAELS ARGENT

MARCH 27-28 *SOLD OUT* JOE COCKER and the GREASE BAND BRIAN AUGER and the TRINITY STONE THE CROWS

APRIL 3-4 QUICKSILVER VAN MORRISON BRINSLEY SCHWARZ

SUNDAY APRIL 5 8:00 PM Only TOM PAXTON Produced in Association with Jay K. Hoffman

THURSDAY APRIL 9 8:30 PM Only PINK FLOYD Produced in Association with Jay K. Hoffman

A rare view of the stage with the light show screen raised exposing the backstage area. Bill Graham at the microphone, May 8, 1970.

Opposite:

A backstage scene after a show, May 23, 1971.

Bill Graham and Grace Slick at a backstage party, May 8, 1970.

Bill Graham yawning after the show on February 11, 1970. Allan Arkush at left, Kip Cohen at right.

View of the orchestra area while the crew adjusts some lights on the front of the balcony. The lighting control booth is clearly visible in the background at right.

Bill Graham with two-year-old son David on his lap during an interview with a journalist, May 15, 1970. This was shot in Graham's upstairs private office.

Kibitzing in the downstairs front office on February 11, 1971. There was always a slightly different atmosphere when Bill Graham was in New York. The staff and crew had to be more on their toes. But when everything was going smoothly there was usually a lot of socializing with "the Boss" and Bill was generous with the perks, including food and drink.

89

Pink Floyd at Fillmore East, September 27, 1970.

Opposite, from top, left to right:

J. Geils Band at Fillmore East, 6/27/71.
James Taylor at Fillmore East, 1/25/71.
Nina Simone at Fillmore East, 5/30/70.
Jerry Lee Lewis at Steve Paul's Scene, 1969.
John Mayall at Fillmore East, 10/4/69.
Rod Stewart & Ron Wood at Fillmore East, Bill Graham in shadows, 2/17/71.

In the summer of 1969 the technical crew rebuilt and extended the front of the stage, ripping out the first three rows of seats to create more space onstage for the performers.

The technical crew built the new sound system on the Fillmore East stage with power woodworking tools and other equipment that Bill Graham bought for the job. They constructed the acoustically designed wooden speaker boxes which were then fitted with Altec Lansing and other components. In this picture the guys are maneuvering one of the newly constructed speakers.

The stage crew making a quick set change using the moving drum kit dollies invented at Fillmore East, February 11, 1970.

The stage crew loading out equipment after a Leon Russell and Taj Mahal weekend, May 23, 1971.

The stage crew playing their favorite game "Noonan Ball," named after crew member John Ford Noonan (with bandana), after a show on April 4, 1970 about 4 a.m.

ON THE ROAD: THE SUMMER OF '69

For me, the "Summer of '69" — the greatest performance summer in rock history — lasted all the way through November of that year; it was a state of mind as much as a calendar time frame. Kicking off in June with a festival in California called Newport '69, through Woodstock in August and the tragedy of Altamont in December, more rock festivals were held in 1969 than in any other year. They attracted a total of more than one million fans in the United States alone and became a musical, sociological — and even political — phenomenon that, along with Vietnam, drugs, and sexual experimentation (all of which, of course, also found their expression at the festivals) defined an entire generation. Like thousands of other long-haired youth, I took to the road, joining what we optimistically called a New Nation, following the music.

Traveling with the Joshua Light Show or with others associated with the Fillmore family, I trekked to sprawling festivals slopped in mud as well as to outdoor concerts and other performance events that were landmarks in the development of rock as a genre. They were also turning points in the transformation of the rock scene from a revolutionary counter-culture adventure to a big bucks commercial establishment saturated by superstars and super egos. I took my cameras everywhere, shooting 16mm color film as well as black & white and color still photos. In July and August I shot the Newport Jazz Festival, Tanglewood, and Woodstock, before flying to England for the Isle of Wight Festival in September. The Who premiering the full live version of their rock opera Tommy at the F.E. in October was another seminal event, and then there was the Rolling Stones tour in November with their Madison Square Garden concert in New York on Thanksgiving Day. The Stones tour culminated little more than a week later in the free concert at California's Altamont Speedway where, as Mick Jagger sang "Sympathy for the Devil," Hells Angels security men stabbed a fan to death in front of the stage, definitively putting an end to any notion of rock innocence.

NEWPORT

The venerable Newport Jazz Festival in Newport, Rhode Island, got its start in the 1950s, and the 1969 edition over the Fourth of July weekend marked the first time that rock groups appeared on the bill alongside jazz and blues greats. Festival director George Wein admitted he was taking a calculated risk with this artistic experiment, but he wanted to introduce his regular festival goers to new forms of music — and also to the visual theatrics of the Joshua Light Show. The line-up was exciting, featuring premier rock acts including James Brown; Sly and the Family Stone; Frank Zappa and the Mothers of Invention; Blood, Sweat and Tears; Ten Years After; Led Zeppelin; and Jethro Tull; side by side with jazz virtuosi like Miles Davis, Dave Brubeck, Rashaan Roland Kirk, and more. Afterward, however, Wein told Downbeat magazine that the experiment was a failure; he called the four-day festival "sheer hell." He hadn't factored-in rock festival hysteria when making his plans. Caught up in the festival phenomenon which had been building through the summer, thousands of young rock fans had converged on Newport without even a bare hope of getting tickets, setting the stage for what became, in one reviewer's words, a "gate-crashing extravaganza." Gates, fences, and barriers were stormed by stampeding fans, seating areas were swamped and total chaos reigned, on and off stage.

Amalie at Woodstock.

The crisis peaked just before Sly and the Family Stone went on, and continued through their set. Cops were everywhere, psyched up to restrain a riot. It was the Fourth of July weekend, and the kids were juiced up on alcohol and undoubtedly other celebratory stimulants. Thousands of fans knocked down the storm fence that separated the audience from the press and photographers' section, where I was standing. We all got knocked over and nearly trampled into the mud. One of my cameras – a borrowed Eclair NPR movie camera that weighed 26 pounds — went flying and I only managed to save it by sticking out my leg to break its fall. I carried the bruises for weeks afterwards. The heavy rain that started midway through Sly's first number only made things worse. Finally, the organizers stopped the show. I feel lucky to have gotten any pictures that day at all, but I think that some of the frenzy, onstage and off, is reflected even in this close-up of Sly.

Among my favorite pictures from Newport is the multiple image color sequence I did of B.B. King; there were so many good shots of him from that concert that I had to put them together — it's almost an animation.

Johnny Winter at Fillmore East, January 11, 1969.

John Sebastian at Tanglewood, July 21, 1970.

B.B. King at the Newport Festival, July 1969.

James Brown at Newport, July 1969.

Miles Davis at Newport, July 1969.

Sly Stone at Newport, July 1969.

The Holiday Inn "Fillmore at Tanglewood" sign, August 12, 1969.

THE FILLMORE AT TANGLEWOOD

Bill Graham produced four concerts in all at Tanglewood, the renowned classical music venue in the Berkshires, an outdoor covered arena with further informal seating on surrounding grassy slopes, which is the summer home of the Boston Symphony Orchestra. The first, billed as "The Fillmore at Tanglewood," took place on August 12, 1969 — just a few days before Woodstock — as part of a new "Contemporary Trends" concert series at the annual Berkshire Music Festival. It was entirely a Fillmore event, staged under the Tanglewood umbrella — Graham not only produced it, but brought the full-scale Fillmore East operation up there, including the Joshua Light Show, to ensure that it would work smoothly from a technical as well as artistic standpoint. The success of this first concert led to three similar events the next summer.

The idea of presenting rock music in a high-brow classical setting and introducing it to new audiences fell well within Bill Graham's goal of mixing musical styles and genres which he carried out with such flair and dedication at the Fillmores. By now, it's commonplace to mix musical venues and genres like this; by 1970 rock groups were already playing Carnegie Hall and the Metropolitan Opera. Bill Graham even showcased classical organist Virgil Fox playing Bach at the F.E. in December 1970,

with Joe's Lights sharing the billing as a featured accompaniment. But that first Tanglewood concert represented a real breakthrough — the mere juxtaposition of the words "Fillmore" and "Tanglewood" in the same breath — or on the same notice board — was, quite simply, extraordinary! In a sense it gave a cultural seal of approval to rock, raising its profile and image as a true art form. It was all very heady to rub shoulders with this world. The night before the concert, a group of us went out to dinner and, shortly after we ordered our meal, Leonard Bernstein came in and was seated at the next table. Through broadcasts, concerts and his own compositions, Bernstein had already done much to raise the public image of rock and popular music. He was fascinated by what we were doing at Tanglewood and leaned over to talk with us. He was disarmingly informal — when my dinner came, he thought it looked good and asked for a taste, which, of course, I gave him.

More than 23,000 mainly young spectators turned out to hear Jefferson Airplane, B.B. King, and The Who — by far the largest audience for any Tanglewood concert up to then — and Bill Graham himself was introduced onstage by composer Gunther Schuller, the head of Tanglewood's contemporary music activities. One reviewer described the crowd as "positively worshipful." B.B. King opened the show, but The Who dominated the concert with a brilliant set, performed without a break, that showcased material from Tommy. Released some months earlier, Tommy had been hailed as a rock classic and had become The Who's first really big smash hit in the U.S. More than that, the Tommy double album represented the most ambitious and sustained creation in the rock idiom to date, adding a new, conceptual dimension to rock as art. Presenting music from Tommy at Tanglewood, thus, did more than capitalize on the rock opera's popularity. It also underscored the creative transitions under way in rock music, and in thinking about rock music, embodied by the entire "Fillmore at Tanglewood" experience.

The concerts the following summer also had exciting, and even more varied, line-ups. John Sebastian, the original tie-dyed hippie from the Lovin' Spoonful, played the July 21, 1970 show — his outfit cried out to be photographed in color! The August 18, 1970 concert was headlined by Santana and featured an inscrutable Miles Davis.

Bill Graham talks to his crew at Tanglewood, August 18, 1970. From left to right: (from back) Ben Haller, Bill Graham, (from back) Bob See, Michael Ahern, (standing) Doug Rye, John Chester, (from back) Arthur Shafransky, Lee Erdman, Ted Abramowitz.

A view from backstage of the Woodstock Festival with the crowd filling up the field while the crew hangs the light show screen, August 13, 1969.

WOODSTOCK

What can I say about Woodstock, "three days of peace, love and music" on Max Yasgur's 600-acre farm in upstate New York, that hasn't already been said, written, or shown on film? The 400,000 crowd; the traffic jams and abandoned cars; the births, the deaths, the mud, the music ... all have become the stuff of legend, a dense, defining moment for the baby-boomer generation. Almost everyone connected with the Fillmore was involved with Woodstock. I went up with The Joshua Light Show. The Light Show was supposed to perform throughout the festival, and we had schlepped four tons of equipment to the site and spent two days setting up the screen and platform. But we only managed a couple brief sets on the first night — the winds that came up with the first rain the next day blew down the screen. Once ensconced behind the stage, though, we were trapped like everyone else. I lucked out by being invited to stay in someone's camper — it was first class comfort; there was even a refrigerator full of steaks that were prepared one night on the BBQ...

I was fascinated by the "how" and "why" of Woodstock, as much as by what was going on onstage. Most of my pictures deal with the crowd, the technical aspect of putting together — and taking down — such a show.

In fact, except for Jefferson Airplane, Canned Heat and one or two other acts, I barely took stills of any of the performances, though I shot 16mm movie footage of Janis Joplin and Jethro Tull. I did a little work for the crew making the Woodstock movie, too, spending hours loading film magazines in a dark recess underneath the stage — which indeed is where I found myself when Jimi Hendrix gave his epic rendition of the Star Spangled Banner, laced throughout with tormented evocations of the Vietnam War. I could hear everything and almost wept because I wasn't out there with my cameras. But I did get a nice photo of Martin Scorsese and Michael Wadleigh in full flush of cinematic battle.

The Woodstock movie crew. From left to right: Michael Wadleigh, Renee Wadleigh, Martin Scorsese, security man.

Canned Heat performing at Woodstock, August 15, 1969.

A backstage view at Woodstock showing the jerryrigged catwalks to the performers' pavilion under construction in the background, August 13, 1969.

The crowd at the Woodstock Festival, August 15, 1969. Every photographer at Woodstock took a version of this picture and I consider myself lucky to have had access to the light show platform, probably the best place there was to shoot from, and where I was standing when I took this using a 135mm lens.

Another backstage view at Woodstock showing the "moat" between the stage and the fence dividing performers and crew from the audience.

The crowd at Woodstock, August 1969. There was a wooden fence around the stage area separating it from the crowds in the field. But enterprising members of the audience sometimes managed to scale it for a better close-up view.

Grace Slick of Jefferson Airplane at Woodstock, August 16, 1969.

The Jefferson Airplane at Woodstock, August 16, 1969.

The aftermath of the Woodstock Festival, August 31, 1969. Technical Director Chris Langhart is standing at left surveying the carnage.

The Who at the Isle of Wight, September 1969.

Actor Terrence Stamp (left) and Manager Albert Grossman (Janis Joplin and Bob Dylan were among his early important clients) in the audience at the Isle of Wight, September 1969.

Scene at the Isle of Wight festival, September 1969.

ISLE OF WIGHT

The Isle of Wight festival was the biggest rock festival in Europe that summer and took place at the beginning of September. I was invited to go with a friend associated with the Fillmore East organization, and I took money out of my savings account to fly over for just three days, arriving in London on the same flight as Bob Dylan and his wife, Sarah, who was then pregnant.

I found the whole scene rather unearthly — maybe because I was jetlagged the entire time. I walked through the crowds and took some pictures of the weird floats and other assemblages people were putting together in the field, and of some of the celebrities in the audience. The first night after we got in, we found ourselves at dinner with a lot of the acts and other people involved with the festival, some of the greatest names in rock, including George Harrison and Dylan and his wife. During the evening, someone started passing around a poster of the event for everyone to sign. I tried to make myself disappear and hoped it would pass me by. But when it stopped at me — I said, "Why not" and signed it with a flourish like everyone else. I've often thought about what happened to that poster, who has it, and if they've ever wondered who "Amalie R. Rothschild" was next to those famous names.

The Who were on the bill; they were everywhere that summer. Roger Daltrey was deep into his chest-baring, fringed buckskin jacket phase; he had already worn the outfit at Tanglewood and Woodstock, and he would still be wearing it in October when the Who premiered *Tommy* at the Fillmore East — but I got my favorite picture of him wearing it at the Isle of Wight. For me, it's definitive Daltrey.

Bob Dylan was THE main attraction of the festival — and he's the one I concentrated on shooting. Dylan had withdrawn from the rock scene and gone into deep seclusion after cracking up his Triumph 55 motorcycle in July 1966 and sustaining critical injuries. He had resumed recording — *John Wesley Harding* came out in 1968 and *Nashville Skyline* was released in May 1969 — and he had even appeared briefly onstage at a memorial concert for Woody Guthrie in January 1968 and, later, at a concert by The Band in the Midwest. The Isle of Wight festival, though, marked Dylan's first full-scale public performance in more than three years — his real return to the spotlight for the first time since the crash, and a quarter of a million people were waiting for this second coming, of sorts. Fans flew in from as far away as California; international rock royalty, including several of the Beatles and Rolling Stones, made sure to be there, too. Dressed in a cream-colored suit and sporting the type of beard later made famous by Yasser Arafat, Dylan took the stage with The Band, and spent an hour spinning out seventeen songs from all stages of his career, including more than half a dozen that

Roger Daltrey at the Isle of Wight, September 1969.

he was performing live for the first time. I had a stage pass and was shooting the show onstage; at one point Robbie Robertson looked straight at me as I clicked the shutter. One of my close-ups of Dylan appeared on the cover of the next issue of Rolling Stone — issue No. 43, October 4, 1969, for which I was paid $30. (I was thrilled, of course, but later I found out that the going rate was $50...)

Although I stopped photographing rock music after the F.E. closed and devoted myself fulltime to filmmaking, Dylan's marathon 1974 tour with The Band, which Bill Graham produced, "brought me out of retirement," and resulted in some of my best pictures of him. John Chester, the Fillmore East's soundman (to whom I was married at the time) designed and built a twenty-four channel mixing console for use on that tour and also went out on the road

as one of the sound engineers. Dylan played thirty-nine concerts in twenty-one cities. I shot pictures at two gigs in the New York area: Madison Square Garden and the Nassau Coliseum on Long Island. Looking back, I was extremely lucky to get such access — twenty million people had tried to get tickets for the 651,000 available seats in all the tour venues.

One picture from the Madison Square Garden concert holds particular meaning for me. I used my 300mm lens, and as I clicked the shutter, I realized I could see myself reflected in Dylan's glasses. If you look closely at the left lens, you can see me, my face obscured by my camera lens, midway from the bottom, to the right of the reflection of the neck of his guitar. His eyes hover behind, looking out and, seemingly, looking far away into the distance.

The Who's drummer Keith Moon at the Isle of Wight Festival, September 1969.

Rick Danko, Bob Dylan and Robbie Robertson at Isle of Wight, September 1969.

Bob Dylan at Nassau Coliseum, January 29, 1974.

Bob Dylan at Isle of Wight, September 1969. This picture was the cover of Rolling Stone No. 43, October 4, 1969.

Bob Dylan at Madison Square Garden, January 31, 1974.

Bob Dylan at Madison Square Garden, January 31, 1974.

The Who performing the "Break the Mirror" sequence of Tommy at Fillmore East, October 24, 1969. Note the shattered mirror effect onscreen. This effect was repeated every night by Tom Shoesmith who created a series of mirrors attached to rubber sheeting which could safely be "broken" performance after performance.

TOMMY

The Who included some of the most flamboyant performers who ever strutted, pranced, smashed their instruments and otherwise let themselves loose on a stage. Pete Townshend's windmill arm and scarecrow figure; Keith Moon going wild on drums; Roger Daltrey, with his naked chest, his chin, his outrageous mane of hair and (of course) his fringed jacket — he was like a mythical romantic centaur rearing back on his hind legs and pawing the air in front of the fans.

The Who was one of the Fillmore East's first headline acts — they topped the bill for two days in April 1968, just two weeks after the venue opened its doors. In October 1969 they appeared at the F.E. for an unprecedented six days in a row, performing their rock opera Tommy in full for the first time in the United States. Throughout the summer they had tantalized audiences around the country with partial versions of the breakthrough oratorio about a blind, deaf and dumb Pin Ball Wizard, and interest was enormous. The F.E. shows were completely sold out far in advance. After all, in popular culture terms, this was history in the making.

I was convinced that we had to make the production really special; we could not just let The Who stand up there onstage and play Tommy as if it were any other concert, with an improvised light show behind them. Not at the Fillmore East, and not with the talents and resources of the Joshua Light Show on hand. Tommy was an opportunity for the light show to devise a special production that worked from a score and libretto and created a complete — live — multimedia experience that would be unique in its scope. I discussed the possibilities for such a production with Joshua White, John Chester, Bob Goddard, Chris Langhart, Bob See, and the other tech staff at the F.E., and they took up the cause with Bill Graham, who enthusiastically allocated $5000 for a production budget out of his profits from the already sold out shows. Graham gave the Light Show prominent billing on the Tommy poster, and included the complete Tommy lyrics in the Fillmore East weekly program for the concerts. The program also listed the names of those of us on the F.E. tech team as "Special Production Staff" for the event.

The special budget, an enormous sum at the time, enabled the crew to build an entirely new light show screen, enlarging it from a thirty-foot flat screen to a curved expanse that stretched fully forty feet across. The curve added new opportunities to distort and play with projected images. The crew also constructed flying mattes which divided the screen visually into separate areas for certain effects created for Tommy. In addition, the money went to augment software and equipment for both the light show and stage lighting.

I was allotted $500 to produce special effects film sequences, notably a wild psychedelic job for the "Acid Queen" number. For this, I used the Light Show's Cecily Hoyt as my actress and filmed her nude, in black & white, walking back and forth across the stage. I filmed the same scene over and over again, using a variety of lenses, camera angles, and speeds, including slow-motion. These were edited into multiple rolls which were then printed down onto one strip of film in four different colors. We used the film in every performance during the six night run — and for the first and only time, I operated equipment during the show, running the 16mm projector from beneath the light show platform, receiving my cues through the intercom headset.

Tommy was an extremely complex and exciting project — by far the most elaborate, sustained light show production undertaken at the F.E. We created our own visual script: a visual score to match the musical score that was repeated, with broad room for improvisation, at each performance. Joshua White stage-managed everything from the wings. Each night as the week went by, the show got more exciting. We could sense the changes, the way things fell tighter and tighter into place in symbiosis with the music. Novel means were used to produce some of the effects. Even the F.E.'s Technical Director, Bob See, got into the act, creating sculptural white flashes of light by using an arc welder to spot weld pieces of metal behind the screen. These bursts of light threw extraordinary shadow shapes from whatever stood between See and the screen.

The crowd at Madison Square Garden, Rolling Stones concert, November 27, 1969.

Janis Joplin backstage with the ghost of Jimi Hendrix at right, Madison Square Garden, November 27, 1969.

Mick Jagger at Madison Square Garden, November 27, 1969.

THANKSGIVING AT MADISON SQUARE GARDEN, November 27, 1969

The Rolling Stones concert at Madison Square Garden on Thanksgiving Day 1969 was one of those events at which everything came together in a way that could not have been planned. The F.E. was closed for the day. As usual, Bill Graham put on a Thanksgiving dinner with all the trimmings for the entire F.E. staff and extended "Fillmore Family" at rows of tables set up in the lobby. Janis Joplin happened to be in town. She was all alone, so of course she was invited for the meal. A bunch of us had tickets for the Stones concert later that evening, and we all went along together. Ike and Tina Turner were the opening act. At some point Tina noticed Janis watching from the wings and invited her onstage to join in on a number.

The resulting shot is probably my favorite out of all the thousands of rock pictures I've taken. I had convinced a security guard to help me get a good position for shooting and used my 300mm lens. For me, time stopped. Look at their expressions! I think it was the only time these two extraordinary rock divas ever sang onstage together — and I only wish I could remember what the song was!

Then the Stones went on. The pictures of Mick Jagger from that concert never fail to astonish me: They capture a fleeting, elusive moment in which he shows a softness and sweetness he rarely ever exposed.

Backstage I captured another remarkable rock moment, without realizing it at the time. I was shooting typical backstage banter — Janis and other performers schmoozing with gaudily dressed fans, friends and hangers-on, while straight-looking security men kept stern watch. Just as I took one shot of Janis in her furry hat, someone walked into the frame, ruining — so I thought — the picture. It wasn't until later, when I was in the darkroom printing the frame, that I saw it was Jimi Hendrix, stepping into the shot toward Janis from who knows where, like a ghostly presence: fuzzy, out of focus, but recognizable. Within a year, both were dead.

Janis Joplin and Tina Turner, Madison Square Garden, November 27, 1969.

Mick Jagger at Madison Square Garden, November 27, 1969.

LAST DANCE

We didn't know it at the time, but the summer of '69 extravaganzas and the success of festivals and big arena concerts helped spell the end for mid-size rock venues like the Fillmore East.

Events like Woodstock and the Isle of Wight made history out of rock music and, for good or bad, put the performers, the fans, the sounds, "the experience" on mainstream magazine covers, TV news shows and movie screens all over the world. The hype made rock musicians and the people around them into national figures. It all happened very quickly. What had felt like a counterculture revolution was being transformed into a social, cultural and even political establishment.

Commercial potential and commercial demands became compelling forces. Superstardom pushed fees higher. Bob Dylan reportedly was paid £35,000 — more than $70,000 — for his hour at the Isle of Wight, compared to well under $10,000 paid to most groups at Woodstock only a couple of weeks before. Big name stars took note. The higher fees forced promoters to focus on bigger, more profitable, high-profile venues and high octane tours. Then there was the labor intensivity of it all: The Stones could play one show at Madison Square Garden and earn as much money — before a bigger crowd — than they would have done with four grueling concerts over two nights at a mid-size hall like the Fillmore East. Ticket prices, too, skyrocketed to meet the higher cost of the acts. The era of "family" was ending and the era of "finance" was on the rise.

For the Fillmore East, it all came to a head in the spring of 1971. Bill Graham dropped the bomb at a hastily called news conference in the F.E. on April 28th. Perched on the edge of the stage, leaning forward into the lights and cameras set up among the plush covered seats in the orchestra section, he announced that he would close down the Fillmore operation on both coasts, starting with the Fillmore East at the end of June.

Graham's announcement was a bitter, personal indictment of changing values in a changing world, of inflated costs, slipping professional standards and lost personal battles. The irony, of course, was that his own success had helped fuel these changes. "Ever since the creation of the Fillmores, it was my sole intention to do nothing more, or less, than present the finest contemporary music in this country, on the best stages and in the most pleasant halls," he said in a statement released at the news conference. "The scene has changed and, in the long run, we are all to one degree or another at fault. All that I know is that what exists now is not what we started with, and what I see around me is less than that with which I prefer to be associated ..."

He railed against a rock scene that had turned into what he called a "music industry of festivals, 20,000-seat halls, miserable production quality, and second-rank promoters." "I am not pleased with this 'music industry,'" he said. "I am not pleased with many of the wealthy musicians working in it, and I am shocked at the nature of the millions of people who support it without asking why."

The developments that led to his decision, Graham said, had been cumulative, but the last straw had been his attempt to cooperate with impresario Sol Hurok in booking a month of rock in the hallowed halls of the Metropolitan Opera. He had been appalled, he said, when the manager for one group — The Band — refused a fee of $50,000 for a week of dates as being too small. "I said Thank You, put down the phone, and that was it," Graham told the news conference.

The announcement hit us in the Fillmore family with the force of a fifty gazilaton bomb. It was the proverbial bolt out of the blue, and we were devastated — we loved the place, the people, the music, the entire scene, and we didn't want it to end.

Nonetheless, I realized that this, too, was part of Fillmore East history — albeit the last chapter — and I decided I would document every facet of the run-up to the June 27 final concert. Since I had studio space on an upper floor of the F.E. building, I was there all the time, and I took hundreds of pictures during those last two months. I wanted to get everything on film, from daily activities and preparations for the closure, to the display case under the marquee listing the programs and ticket sales policy, to the final concert itself. It would be, after all, the ending of an era. Everyone wanted to be there for the finish, and ticket sales for many of the last concerts were limited to ten tickets per purchaser. Admission to the final concert itself was by invitation only.

For the F.E. staff, it was a surreal, feverish time — a strange parody of business as usual. Perhaps no image captures the strangeness better than the photo I shot of two very different people looking at the showcases advertising the last series of concerts. I have no idea who the man in the bowler hat was — William Burroughs perhaps...?

Musically, the Fillmore East went out with a bang. A thrilling series of concerts spanned the final month, each one part of a countdown to blastoff.

The amazingly gifted Laura Nyro, with her searing,

Bill Graham's press conference during which he announced the closing of both Fillmores, April 28, 1971.

soulful voice headlined the bill on May 30. Whenever Laura played the F.E. there was a special atmosphere — a real lovefest between her, the audience, and her eerily emotional music. Hovering over her piano, with her long black hair flowing, she was a haunted, and haunting, presence. Frank Zappa and the Mothers of Invention played June 5 and 6 — the June 5 concert was the one at which John Lennon and Yoko Ono were in the audience for the second show and at two o'clock in the morning joined the Mothers onstage for an encore. The Byrds were the headline act on June 9, and Elton John made a special appearance.

June 27 finally arrived, and we all lived it in a kind of a trance. The day seemed endless, but somehow it still passed in the blink of an eye. The invitations described the final Fillmore East evening as a "concert celebration" featuring "Food, Drink and Joy" as well as music; a single

red rose was placed on each seat in the house. Seven groups and guest artists took the stage — a rock festival in itself: the Allman Brothers, Albert King, the J. Geils Band, the Beach Boys, Country Joe, Mountain and Edgar Winter. Though the event was invitation-only, it was broadcast live, in toto, on WNEW-FM radio. Except for the Beach Boys, the artists were all popular F.E. veterans, favorites with the staff and with the audience. In fact, the final concert was only the second time that the Beach Boys played the F.E. They were bearded and scruffy looking in those waning days of the psychedelic era, not the squeakily clean-cut California surfers they started out to be. I love the picture I got of a pensive Bill Graham watching them from the wings — I'll always wonder what he was thinking. The concert celebration went on until dawn; afterward, we probably all went next door for breakfast at Ratner's, but this is one morning I simply don't remember.

The Who at Tanglewood, July 7, 1970.

Santana at Tanglewood, August 18, 1970.

Final marquee, front view.

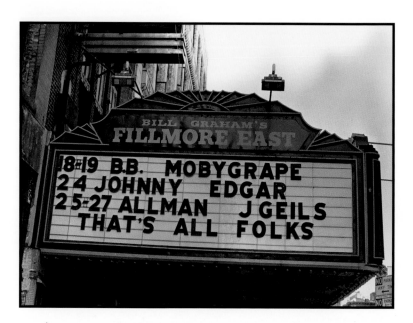

Final marquee, side view.

The west side of the block of Second Avenue between 7th and 6th Streets. The long white-colored building adjacent to the Fillmore East is still known as "Central Plaza" and housed the NYU School of the Arts dance, theater and film programs.

Opposite:

The Who play their rock opera ,Tommy, for the first time in the U.S. at Fillmore East for six nights, October 20–25, 1969.

Miles Davis at Tanglewood, August 18, 1970.

The final showcases under the marquee listing the last series of concerts, May 1971.

The Allman brothers, Duane standing with guitar and Gregg at keyboards, backstage during the afternoon before the last show, June 27, 1971.

Albert King with Joe's Lights background at the last concert at Fillmore East, June 27, 1971.

Ushers counting ticket stubs in the staff lounge.

The staff at an after-show breakfast at Ratner's Dairy Restaurant next door to the Fillmore East, 5 a.m. on a date unknown.

Farewell, late afternoon, June 27, 1971.

The roses on each seat at the last show, June 27, 1971.

Bill Graham watches the Beach Boys from the wings during the last concert, June 27, 1971.

The Fillmore East staff gathered onstage, Bill Graham at microphone, at the end of the very last show, June 27, 1971.

A demonstration of making light show 16mm scratch film loops.

AFTERWORD

This book is the culmination of years of work and years of passion; years of friendship and years of reflection. The Fillmore East was a catalyst for a special type of creativity, and I feel privileged and proud to have been part of the Fillmore Family. Looking back over three decades, I find it hard to believe that the Fillmore experience lasted such a brief period of time. Those few short years at the end of the '60s and beginning of the '70s were a true launching pad for careers and relationships that have developed and deepened over the years. Even though I stopped photographing the rock scene after the F.E. closed, the network of friends and contacts I made there, and the skills, knowledge and attitudes I acquired, have had a powerful and enduring impact on my work.

I have wanted to produce a book on the Fillmore East for many years, but I seriously started preparing material for it in the early 1990s, around the time of Bill Graham's tragic death in a helicopter crash in 1991. Graham's death was a catalyst for my work in reexamining the Fillmore East phenomenon, and his unique vision in creating the F.E. in many ways inspires these pages. It goes without saying that I could not have produced this book alone. On the contrary! While I shot and produced every picture, each photo records a unique symbiosis of talent and energy. With this book I want to pay tribute to each person who appears in each frame, and to many others who do not. I give thanks and credit, too, to all the many people who have helped nurture this project at all stages of its development. They sustained me and believed in me, jogged my memory, scoffed at my doubts and put up with me -- and I could not have done it without them.

I would like to thank a number of people in particular for their aid, support, and friendship. My 1969 run-in with Jerry Pompili, the one-time F.E. house manager, was responsible for my getting a job at the F.E. in the first place. In his later capacity as Vice President of Bill Graham Presents, Jerry has been unstinting with his time, advice and assistance. Rebecca Nichols, the Head of Archives at Bill Graham Presents, has also been incredibly helpful and encouraging. I'm deeply grateful to British Rock Historian John Platt, who in innumerable ways helped shape this book in its early stages. Nathan Farb has been consistently supportive and offered valuable constructive criticism, as have my dear friends Julie Sloane, Josie Dean, Nancy Jervis, Gianna Pontecorboli, Marina Paris and Nadia Werba. Thanks, too, to Bob Herman, Denise Di Carli, Joanne Morgante, Kevin Walz, Jane Colman & Don Watson, Catherine Ventura, Ed Apfel, Mirra Bank and the staff at Acid Test — Designer Michael Quinn, Operations Manager Barbara Quinn, Production Head Linda Karr and Editor Sherry Sterling. I could not have done anything at all without my four darkroom and office assistants over the years, Sarah Douglas, Jessica Burko, Giulia Ceccacci and Katherine Shamraj. Likewise, I owe a special debt of friendship, gratitude and respect to Carolyn Strachan who has run my New York life and business since 1982. My lawyer Karen Shatzkin has been a firm friend and trusted advisor who has also been lavish with her moral support. Barry Podgorsky, Sidney Monroe, and Monica Pollock of the SoHo Triad Gallery in New York have demonstrated their belief in me and my work by representing me in a way which has brought me pride as well as recognition. And I want to pay special tribute to Josh Hanig, filmmaker and friend extraordinaire who, sadly, left us before this book came to fruition: I miss you, Josh.

As I worked on this book, I reconnected with many other people associated with the Fillmore who provided vital links with the past, whether in formal interviews, or in informal memory-racking sessions. Some gave much needed help in identifying people in the photos! Many appear in the photographs and are mentioned in the text; others do not. I would like to express a deep sense of gratitude to them all, in alphabetical order: Michael Ahern, Allan Arkush, Al Aronowitz, Jancy Ball, Jay Benzon, Candace Brightman, Bruce Byall, Marylou Capes, John Chester, Kip Cohen, Jon Davison, Maureen Devlin, George Eichen, Stephen Gagne, Jane Geraghty, Bob Goddard, Ben Haller, Jake Haselkorn, Cecily Hoyt Jaffe, Keith Kevan, Michael Klenfner, Chris Langhart, Alan Mande, Barry Melton, John Morris, Mark Morris, David Noffsinger, Dan Opatoshu, Sydney Michael Rogers, Doug Rye, Stanley Schnier, Fred Schwartz, Bob See, Thomas Shoesmith, David Vartanoff, Joshua White, John Zacherle, and Gail Rodgers Zecker.

My family has been an invaluable source of strength and love throughout this project, as throughout my life. My parents in particular have backed me every step of the way and have always been there for me. My cousins, Richard and Giovanna Schamberg, have provided a welcoming base for me on the West Coast. Finally, I would like to thank three people who helped take my dreams and actually translate them into this book: Stacy Kreutzmann Quinn and Nancy Reid, my editors and publishers at Acid Test Productions, who believed in this project and had the courage to take it on, and Ruth Ellen Gruber, who got me to say what I wanted to say.

— ARR

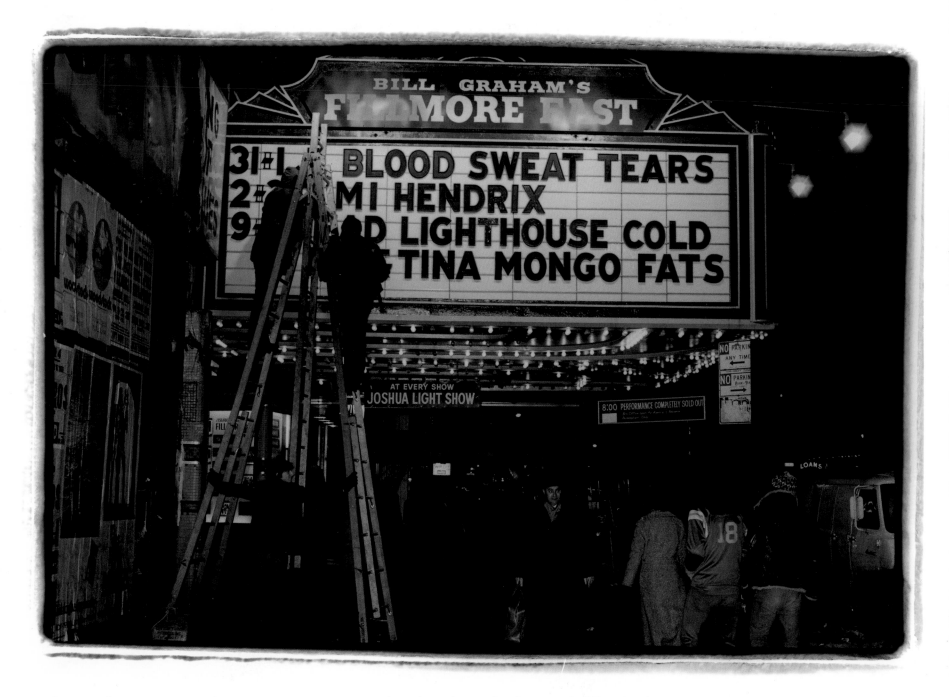

Changing the marquee, December 28, 1969. Note "At every show the Joshua Light Show" suspended under the marquee.

BILL GRAHAM PRESENTS EAST COAST SHOW LIST MARCH 8, 1968 THROUGH JUNE 27, 1971

All venues Fillmore East unless noted otherwise

Date	Performer 1	Performer 2	Performer 3	Notes
Fri. 3/8/68	Big Brother with Janis Joplin	Tim Buckley	Albert King	2 shows Albert King's drummer was in the Army AWOL. The Military Police showed up and took him away.
Fri. 3/22/68	Doors	ARS Nova	Crome Syrcus	2 shows
Sat. 3/23/68	Doors	ARS Nova	Crome Syrcus	2 shows
Fri. 3/29/68	Richie Havens	Troggs	United States of America	2 shows
Sat. 3/30/68	Richie Havens	Troggs	United States of America	2 shows
Fri. 4/5/68	The Who	Buddy Guy	Free Spirits	2 shows
Sat. 4/6/68	The Who	Buddy Guy	Free Spirits	2 shows
Fri. 4/12/68	Butterfield Blues Band	Charles Lloyd	Tom Rush	2 shows
Sat. 4/13/68	Butterfield Blues Band	Charles Lloyd	Tom Rush	2 shows
Fri. 5/19/68	Mothers of Invention	James Cotton		2 shows: Last NY appearance 'till peace
Sat. 4/20/68	Mothers of Invention	James Cotton		2 shows: Last NY appearance 'till peace
Fri. 4/26/68	Traffic	Blue Cheer	Iron Butterfly	2 shows
Sat. 4/27/68	Traffic	Blue Cheer	Iron Butterfly	2 shows
Fri. 5/3/68	Jefferson Airplane	Crazy World of Arthur Brown		2 shows
Sat. 5/4/68	Jefferson Airplane	Crazy World of Arthur Brown		2 shows
Fri. 5/10/68	Jimi Hendrix	Sly & Family Stone		2 shows
Sat. 5/11/68	Auto Salvage	Group Therapy	Joyfull Noise	2 shows
Fri. 5/17/68	Byrds	Tim Buckley	Foundations	2 shows
Sat. 5/18/68	Byrds	Tim Buckley	Foundations	2 shows
Fri. 5/24/68	Ravi Shankar	Alla Rakah		
Sat. 5/25/68	Country Joe & The Fish	Blue Cheer	Pigmeat Markham	
Fri. 5/31/68	Moby Grape	Fugs	Gary Burton Quartet	2 shows
Sat. 6/1/68	Moby Grape	Fugs	Gary Burton Quartet	2 shows
Sun. 6/2/68	Bill Cosby	Janice Ian	Frankie Dunlop & Maletta	Also: Jazz Pantomime salute to Dick Gregory
Fri. 6/7/68	Electric Flag	Quicksilver	Steppenwolf	2 shows
Sat. 6/8/68	Electric Flag	Quicksilver	Steppenwolf	2 shows
Fri. 6/14/68	Grateful Dead	Jeff Beck	Seventh Sons	2 shows
Sat. 6/15/68	Grateful Dead	Jeff Beck	Seventh Sons	2 shows
Fri. 6/21/68	Vanilla Fudge	James Cotton	Loading Zone	2 shows
Sat. 6/22/68	Georgie Fame	James Cotton	Loading Zone	2 shows
Fri. 7/19/68	Jefferson Airplane	H.P. Lovecraft		2 shows
Sat. 7/29/68	Jefferson Airplane	H.P. Lovecraft		2 shows
Fri. 8/2/68	Big Brother	Staple Singers	Ten Years After	2 shows
Sat. 8/3/68	Big Brother	Staple Singers	Ten Years After	2 shows
Fri. 8/9/68	Joan Baez			
Sat. 8/10/68	Joan Baez			
Fri. 9/13/68	Chambers Brothers	Blood Sweat and Tears	Amboy Dukes	2 shows
Sat. 9/14/68	Chambers Brothers	Blood Sweat and Tears	Amboy Dukes	2 shows
Fri. 9/20/68	Traffic	Staple Singers	Crome Syrcus	2 shows
Sat. 9/21/68	Traffic	Staple Singers	Crome Syrcus	2 shows
Fri. 9/27/68	Country Joe & The Fish	Ten Years After	Procol Harum	
Sat. 9/28/68	Country Joe & The Fish	Ten Years After	Procol Harum	

Fri. 10/4/68	Eric Burden & The Animals	Sly & The Family Stone	Lynn County	
Sat. 10/5/68	Eric Burden & The Animals	Sly & The Family Stone	Lynn County	
Fri. 10/11/68	Beach Boys	Creedence Clearwater Revival		2 shows
Sat. 10/12/68	Turtles	Creedence Clearwater Revival	New York Rock & Roll Ensemble	2 shows
Fri. 10/18/68	Jeff Beck	Tim Buckley	Albert King	2 shows
Sat. 10/19/68	Jeff Beck	Tim Buckley	Albert King	2 shows
Fri. 10/25/68	Moody Blues	John Mayall	Rhinoceros	2 shows
Sat. 10/26/68	Moody Blues	John Mayall	Rhinoceros	2 shows
Fri. 11/1/68	Richie Havens	Quicksilver	McCoys	2 shows
Sat. 11/2/68	Richie Havens	Quicksilver	The Move	2 shows
Fri. 11/8/68	Steppenwolf	Buddy Rich	Children of God	2 shows Children of God replaced The Move who cancelled
Sat. 11/9/68	Steppenwolf	Buddy Rich	Children of God	2 shows Children of God replaced The Move who cancelled
Fri. 11/15/68	Country Joe & The Fish			2 shows
Sat. 11/16/68	Country Joe & The Fish			2 shows
Fri. 11/22/68	Iron Butterfly	Canned Heat	Youngbloods	2 shows
Sat. 11/23/68	Iron Butterfly	Canned Heat	Youngbloods	2 shows
Wed. 11/27/68	Incredible String Band			
Thur. 11/28/68	Jefferson Airplane	Buddy Guy	Chuck Davis Dance Co.	2 shows
Fri. 11/29/68	Jefferson Airplane	Buddy Guy	Chuck Davis Dance Co.	2 shows
Sat. 11/30/68	Jefferson Airplane	Buddy Guy	Chuck Davis Dance Co.	2 shows
Wed. 11/4/68	Duke Ellington	New York Rock & Roll Ensemble		benefit for Odyssey House
Thur. 12/5/68	H. Rap Brown/ Bernadine Dohrn	Herbert Marcuse	Carl Oglesby /Pete Seger	Radical Perspectives benefit for the Guardian Newspaper
Fri. 12/6/68	Country Joe & The Fish	Fleetwood Mac	Kusama's Self-Obliteration	2 shows
Sat. 12/7/68	Country Joe & The Fish	Fleetwood Mac	Kusama's Self-Obliteration	2 shows
Fri. 12/13/68	Sam & Dave Review	Super Session	Earth Opera	Super Session with Mike Bloomfield & Al Kooper
Sat. 12/14/68	Sam & Dave Review	Super Session	Earth Opera	Super Session with Mike Bloomfield & Al Kooper
Fri. 12/20/68	Creedence Clearwater Revival	Deep Purple	James Cotton Blues Band	2 shows
Sat. 12/21/68	Creedence Clearwater Revival	Deep Purple	James Cotton Blues Band	2 shows
Fri. 12/27/68	Butterfield Blues Band	Crazy World of Arthur Brown	Super Session /Sweetwater	2 shows: also Sweetwater, Super Session included, Bloomfield, Kooper, and friends
Sat. 12/28/68	Butterfield Blues Band	Crazy World of Arthur Brown	Super Session /Sweetwater	2 shows: also Super Session included Bloomfield, Kooper, and friends
Sun. 12/29/68	Walter Carlos /ARS Nova	Good Earth/ American Brass Quintet	New York Rock & Roll Ensemble / New YorkElectric St. Ensemble	"An Eclectic Christmas" Musical Coordinators, John E & George F. Sackert
Tue. 12/31/68	Chambers Brothers	Mother Earth		2 shows
Fri. 1/10/69	B.B. King	Winter with Johnny Winter	Terry Reid	2 shows
Sat. 1/11/69	B.B. King	Winter with Johnny Winter	Terry Reid	2 shows
Fri. 1/17/69	Buddy Rich	Grass Roots	Spirit	2 shows
Sat. 1/18/69	Buddy Rich	Grass Roots	Spirit	2 shows
Fri. 1/24/69	Blood Sweat & Tears	Jethro Tull	Gay Desperados Steel Band	2 shows: Gay Desperados Steel Band replaced Savoy Brown Blues Band
Sat. 1/25/69	Blood Sweat & Tears	Jethro Tull	Gay Desperados Steel Band	2 shows: Gay Desperados Steel Band replaced Savoy Brown Blues Band
Fri. 1/31/69	Iron Butterfly	Led Zeppelin	Porter's Popular Preachers	2 shows The Move replaced by Porter's Popular Preachers
Sat. 2/1/69	Iron Butterfly	Led Zeppelin	Porter's Popular Preachers	2 shows The Move replaced by Porter's Popular Preachers

Date	Headliner			Notes
Fri. 2/7/69	Canned Heat	Pentangle	Rhinoceros	2 shows
Sat. 2/8/69	Canned Heat	Pentangle	Rhinoceros	2 shows
Tues. 2/11/69	Grateful Dead	Janis Joplin		2 shows
Wed. 2/12/69	Grateful Dead	Janis Joplin		2 shows
Fri. 2/14/69	Sam & Dave	Winter	Aorta	2 shows: Winter replaces Small Faces, Sam & Dave replaced Jeff Beck
Sat. 2/15/69	Chuck Berry	Winter	Savoy Brown Aorta	2 shows: Winter replaced Small Faces, Chuck Berry replaced Jeff Beck
Fri. 2/21/69	Mothers of Invention	Buddy Miles Express	Chicago Transit Authority	2 shows
Sat. 2/22/69	Mothers of Invention	Buddy Miles Express	Chicago Transit Authority	2 shows
Fri. 2/28/69	Ten Years After	John Mayall	Slim Harpo	2 shows
Sat. 3/1/69	Ten Years After	John Mayall	Slim Harpo	2 shows
Fri. 3/7/69	Buffy Sainte-Marie	Ian & Sylvia	Great Speckled Bird	
Sat. 3/8/69	Vanilla Fudge	Amboy Dukes	Sirocco	
Fri. 3/14/69	Procol Harum	Pacific Gas & Electric	The Collectors	
Sat. 3/15/69	Procol Harum	Pacific Gas & Electric	The Collectors	
Fri. 3/21/69	Creedence Clearwater Revival	Spirit	Aynsley Dunbar Retaliation	
Sat. 3/22/69	Creedence Clearwater Revival	Spirit	Aynsley Dunbar Retaliation	
Fri. 3/28/69	Steppenwolf	Julie Driscoll, Brian Auger and the Trinity	John Hammond	2 shows
Sat. 3/29/69	Steppenwolf	Julie Driscoll, Brian Auger and the Trinity	John Hammond	2 shows
Fri. 4/4/69	Chambers Brothers	Hello People	Elephant's Memory	2 shows
Sat. 4/5/69	Chambers Brothers	Hello People	Elephant's Memory	2 shows
Wed. 4/8/69	Ten Years After	The Nice	Family	2 shows
Thur. 4/9/69	Ten Years After	The Nice	Family	2 shows
Fri. 4/11/69	Blood Sweat and Tears	Jethro Tull; Albert King	AUM	2 shows Albert King replaces Jethro Tull on late show
Sat. 4/12/69	Blood Sweat and Tears	Jethro Tull; Savoy Brown	AUM	2 shows Savoy Brown replaces Jethro Tull on late show
Fri. 4/18/69	Butterfield Blues Band	Foundations	Savoy Brown	2 shows
Sat. 4/19/69	Butterfield Blues Band	Foundations	Savoy Brown	2 shows
Fri. 4/25/69	Joni Mitchell	James Cotton	Taj Mahal	2 shows
Sat. 4/26/69	Joni Mitchell	James Cotton	Taj Mahal	2 shows
Sun. 4/27/69	Incredible String Band			
Fri. 5/2/69	Jeff Beck	Joe Cocker & Grease Band	NRBQ	2 shows
Sat. 5/3/69	Jeff Beck	Joe Cocker & Grease Band	NRBQ	2 shows
Fri. 5/9/69	The Band	Cat Mother & the Allnight Newsboys		2 shows
Sun. 5/11/69	Incredible String Band			
Fri. 3/16/69	The Who	Sweetwater	It's A Beautiful Day	2 shows: There was a fire at the store on the corner and the building had to be evacuated.
Sat. 3/17/69	The Who	Sweetwater	It's A Beautiful Day	2 shows
Sun. 3/18/69	The Who	Sweetwater	It's A Beautiful Day	
Fri. 5/23/69	Sly & The Family Stone	Clarence Carter	Rotary Connection	2 shows
Sat. 5/24/69	Sly & The Family Stone	Clarence Carter	Rotary Connection	2 shows
Thur. 5/29/69	Led Zeppelin	Woody Herman & His Orchestra	Delaney & Bonnie	2 shows

Fri. 5/30/69	Led Zeppelin	Woody Herman & His Orchestra	Delaney & Bonnie	2 shows
Sat. 5/31/69	Led Zeppelin	Woody Herman & His Orchestra	Delaney & Bonnie	2 shows
Fri. 6/6/69	Chuck Berry	Albert King		2 shows
Sat. 6/7/69	Chuck Berry	Albert King		2 shows
Fri. 6/13/69	Booker T. & The M.G.'s	Youngbloods	Chicago	2 shows
Sat. 6/14/69	Booker T. & The M.G.'s	Youngbloods	Chicago	2 shows
Fri. 6/20/69	Grateful Dead	Buddy Miles Express		2 shows
Sat. 6/21/69	Grateful Dead	Buddy Miles Express		2 shows
Fri. 6/27/69	Procol Harum	Byrds	Raven	2 shows
Sat. 6/28/69	Procol Harum	Byrds	Raven	2 shows
Thur. 7/3/69	Jeff Beck Group	Jethro Tull	Soft White Underbelly	2 shows
Fri. 7/4/69	Iron Butterfly	Blues Image	Man	2 shows
Sat. 7/5/69	Iron Butterfly	Blues Image	Man	Saturday late show cancelled
Fri. 7/11/69	John Mayall	Preservation Hall Jazz Band	Spooky Tooth	2 shows
Sat. 7/12/69	John Mayall	Preservation Hall Jazz Band	Spooky Tooth	2 shows
Fri. 7/18/69	Creedence Clearwater Revival	Terry Reid	AUM	2 shows
Sat. 7/19/69	Creedence Clearwater Revival	Terry Reid	AUM	2 shows
Fri. 8/1/69	Canned Heat	Three Dog Night	Santana/ Sha-Na-Na (late show only)	2 shows
Sat. 8/2/69	Canned Heat	Three Dog Night	Santana/ Sha-Na-Na (late show only)	2 shows
Fri. 8/8/69	Jefferson Airplane	Joe Cocker & Grease Band	Spontaneous Sound	
Sat. 8/9/69	Jefferson Airplane	Joe Cocker & Grease Band	Spontaneous Sound	
Tue. 8/12/69 Tanglewood	Jefferson Airplane	B.B. King	The Who	also: Christopher Tree's Spontaneous Sound
Thur. 9/4/69	Incredible String Band			
Fri. 9/5/69	B.B. King	Albert King	Bobby Blue Band	2 shows
Sat. 9/6/69	B.B. King	Albert King	Bobby Blue Band	2 shows
Sun. 9/7/69	Ravi Shankar			
Fri. 9/12/69	Ten Years After	Mother Earth	Flock	2 shows
Sat. 9/13/69	Ten Years After	Mother Earth	Flock	2 shows
Sun. 9/14/69	Incredible String Band			
Fri. 9/19/69	Crosby, Stills, Nash & Young	Lonnie Mack		2 shows
Sat. 9/20/69	Crosby, Stills, Nash & Young	Lonnie Mack		2 shows
Fri. 9/26/69	Country Joe & The Fish	Grateful Dead	Sha-Na-Na	2 shows
Sat. 9/27/69	Country Joe & The Fish	Grateful Dead	Sha-Na-Na	2 shows
Fri. 10/3/69	Chuck Berry	John Mayall	Elvin Bishop Group	2 shows
Sat. 10/4/69	Chuck Berry	John Mayall	Elvin Bishop Group	2 shows
Fri. 10/10/69	Vanilla Fudge	Dr. John the Night Tripper		
Sat.10/11/69	Vanilla Fudge	Dr. John the Night Tripper		
Fri. 10/17/69	Spirit	Kinks	Bonzo Dog Band	2 shows
Sat. 10/18/69	Spirit	Kinks	Bonzo Dog Band	2 shows
Mon. 10/20/69	The Who	King Crimson	AUM	The Who perform *Tommy*
Tues. 10/21/69	The Who	King Crimson	AUM	The Who perform *Tommy*
Wed. 10/22/69	The Who	King Crimson	AUM	The Who perform *Tommy*
Thur. 10/23/69	The Who	King Crimson	AUM	The Who perform *Tommy*
Fri. 10/24/69	The Who	King Crimson	AUM	The Who perform *Tommy*
Sat. 10/25/69	The Who	King Crimson	AUM	The Who perform *Tommy*
Tues. 10/28/69	Tuesday Night Jam			"Tuesday Night Auditions and Jams" advertised at least through end of year
Fri. 10/31/69	Mountain	Steve Miller Band	The Move	2 shows

Date	Headliner	Support	Support	Notes
Sat. 11/1/69	Mountain	Steve Miller Band	The Move	2 shows
Fri. 11/7/69	Santana	Butterfield Blues Band	Humble Pie	2 shows
Sat. 11/8/69	Santana	Butterfield Blues Band	Humble Pie	2 shows
Fri. 11/14/69	Johnny Winter	Chicago	Blodwyn Pig	2 shows
Sat. 11/15/69	Johnny Winter	Chicago	Blodwyn Pig	2 shows
Fri. 11/21/69	Joe Cocker & Grease Band	Fleetwood Mac	King Crimson /Voices of East Harlem	Voices of East Harlem perform at late show
Sat. 11/22/69	Joe Cocker & Grease Band	Fleetwood Mac	King Crimson /Voices of East Harlem	Voices of East Harlem perform at late show
Wed. 11/26/69	Jefferson Airplane	Youngbloods	Joseph Egers Crossover	2 shows
Fri. 11/28/69	Jefferson Airplane	Youngbloods	Joseph Egers Crossover	2 shows
Sat. 11/29/69	Jefferson Airplane	Youngbloods	Joseph Egers Crossover	2 shows
Fri. 12/5/69	Jethro Tull	Grand Funk Railroad	Fat Mattress	2 shows
Sat. 12/6/69	Jethro Tull	Grand Funk Railroad	Fat Mattress	2 shows
Fri. 12/12/69	Richie Havens	Nina Simone		2 shows
Sat. 12/13/69	Richie Havens	Nina Simone		2 shows
Sun. 12/14/69	Incredible String Band			produced with Jay K. Hoffman
Fri. 12/19/69	Byrds	Nice	Sons of Champlin	2 shows: Dion at late show
Sat. 12/20/69	Byrds	Nice	Sons of Champlin	2 shows: Dion at late show
Fri. 12/26/69	Blood Sweat and Tears	Appaloosa	Allman Brothers	2 shows
Sat. 12/27/69	Blood Sweat and Tears	Appaloosa	Allman Brothers	2 shows
Sun. 12/28/69	Blood Sweat and Tears	Appaloosa	Allman Brothers	2 shows
Wed. 12/31/69	Jimi Hendrix	Voices of East Harlem		2 shows
Thurs. 1/1/70	Jimi Hendrix	Voices of East Harlem		2 shows
Fri. 1/2/70	Grateful Dead	Lighthouse	Cold Blood	2 shows
Sat. 1/3/70	Grateful Dead	Lighthouse	Cold Blood	2 shows
Fri. 1/9/70	Ike & Tina Turner	Mongo Santamaria	Fats Domino	2 shows
Sat. 1/10/70	Ike & Tina Turner	Mongo Santamaria	Fats Domino	2 shows
Fri. 1/16/70	Santana	Catfish		2 shows
Sat. 1/17/70	Santana	Catfish		2 shows
Fri. 1/23/70	Quicksilver	Country Joe & The Fish	Eric Mercury	2 shows
Sat. 1/24/70	Quicksilver	Country Joe & The Fish	Eric Mercury	2 shows
Fri. 1/30/70	Mountain	Jack Bruce & Friends		2 shows
Sat. 1/31/70	Mountain	Jack Bruce & Friends		2 shows
Fri. 2/6/70	Delaney & Bonnie & Friends	Seals & Crofts	Eric Clapton	2 shows D & B play with Eric Clapton
Sat. 2/7/70	Delaney & Bonnie & Friends	Seals & Crofts	Eric Clapton	2 shows D & B play with Eric Clapton
Wed. 2/11/70	Allman Brothers	Grateful Dead	Love	2 shows jam with Mick Fleetwood
Fri. 2/13/70	Allman Brothers	Grateful Dead	Love	2 shows
Sat. 2/14/70	Allman Brothers	Grateful Dead	Love	2 shows
Fri. 2/20/70	Savoy Brown	Kinks	Renaissance /Noonan	2 shows
Sat. 2/21/70	Savoy Brown	Kinks	Renaissance /Noonan	2 shows
Sun. 2/22/70	Ravi Shankar			with Zakir Quereshi – Tabla Dr. Ashoka Ray – Tambora
Thur. 2/26/70	Ten Years After	Zephyr	John Hammond	
Fri. 2/27/70	Ten Years After	Doug Kershaw	Zephyr	
Sat. 2/28/70	Ten Years After	Doug Kershaw	Zephyr	
Fri. 3/6/70	Neil Young & Crazy Horse	Steve Miller Blues Band	Miles Davis	2 shows

145

Sat. 3/7/70	Neil Young & Crazy Horse	Steve Miller Blues Band	Miles Davis	2 shows
Fri. 3/13/70	John Mayall	B.B. King	Taj Mahal	2 shows
Sat. 3/14/70	John Mayall	B.B. King	Taj Mahal	2 shows
Sun. 3/15/70	John Mayall	Taj Mahal	Leon Thomas	
Thur. 3/19/70	Moody Blues	Lee Michaels	Argent	
Fri. 3/20/70	Moody Blues	Lee Michaels	Argent	2 shows
Sat. 3/21/70	Moody Blues	Lee Michaels	Argent	2 shows
Fri. 3/27/70	Joe Cocker, Mad Dogs & Englishmen	Ronnie Hawkins	Stone the Crows	2 shows. Ronnie Hawkins replaced Brian Auger and the Trinity
Sat. 3/28/70	Joe Cocker, Mad Dogs & Englishmen	Ronnie Hawkins	Stone the Crows	2 shows. Ronnie Hawkins replaced Brian Auger and the Trinity
Fri. 4/3/70	Quicksilver Messenger Service	Van Morrison	Brinsley Schwartz	2 shows
Sat. 4/4/70	Quicksilver Messenger Service	Van Morrison	Brinsley Schwartz	2 shows
Sun. 4/5/70	Tom Paxton	Fraser & Debolt		produced with Jay K. Hoffman. Paxton accompanied by David Horowitz
Fri. 4/10/70	Santana	It's a Beautiful Day	American Dream	2 shows: American Dream replaced Free
Sat. 4/11/70	Santana	It's a Beautiful Day	American Dream	2 shows: American Dream replaced Free
Sun. 4/12/70	Santana	It's a Beautiful Day	American Dream	2 shows: American Dream replaced Free
Fri. 4/17/70	Ray Charles	Dizzy Gillespie	Mongo Santamaria	2 shows
Sat. 4/18/70	Ray Charles	Dizzy Gillespie	Mongo Santamaria	2 shows
Thur. 4/23/70	Incredible String Band	Stone Monkey Mime Troupe		"U" - a pop pantomime produced with Jay K. Hoffman
Fri. 4/24/70	Incredible String Band	Stone Monkey Mime Troupe		"U"- a pop pantomime produced with Jay K. Hoffman
Sat. 4/25/70	Incredible String Band	Stone Monkey Mime Troupe		"U"- a pop pantomime produced with Jay K. Hoffman
Sun. 4/26/70	Incredible String Band	Stone Monkey Mime Troupe		"U" - a pop pantomime produced with Jay K. Hoffman
Fri. 5/1/70	Mountain	Blodwyn Pig		2 shows
Sat. 5/2/70	Mountain	Blodwyn Pig		2 shows
Wed. 5/6/70	Jefferson Airplane	Manfred Mann: Chapter 3		2 shows. moved from 4/28 - 29, 1970
Thur. 5/7/70	Jefferson Airplane	Manfred Mann: Chapter 3		2 shows. moved from 4/28 - 29, 1970
Fri. 5/8/70	Mothers of Invention	Insect Trust	Sea Train	2 shows. The Nice cancelled
Sat. 5/9/70	Mothers of Invention	Insect Trust	Sea Train	2 shows. The Nice cancelled
Sun. 5/10/70	Music Festival '70			satellite colorcast from London 3pm-- 8pm delayed broadcast produced with Jay K. Hoffman
Fri. 5/15/70	Grateful Dead	New Riders of the Purple Sage		
Sat. 5/16/70	Guess Who	Cold Blood	Buddy Miles	
Thurs. 5/21/70	Jethro Tull	Clouds	John Sebastian	2 shows
Fri. 5/2270	Jethro Tull	Clouds	John Sebastian	2 shows
Sat. 5/23/70	Jethro Tull	Clouds	John Sebastian	2 shows
Fri. 5/29/70	Nina Simone	Mongo Santamaria	Isaac Hayes	2 shows
Sat. 5/30/70	Nina Simone	Mongo Santamaria	Isaac Hayes	2 shows
Tues. 6/2/70	Crosby, Stills, Nash and Young	Taylor & Reeves		
Wed. 6/3/70	Crosby, Stills, Nash and Young	Taylor & Reeves		
Thur. 6/4/70	Crosby, Stills, Nash and Young	Taylor & Reeves		
Fri. 6/5/70	Crosby, Stills, Nash and Young	Taylor & Reeves		
Sat. 6/6/70	Crosby, Stills, Nash and Young	Taylor & Reeves		
Sun. 6/7/70	Crosby, Stills, Nash and Young	Taylor & Reeves		
Wed. 6/10/70	Traffic	Fairport Convention	Mott the Hoople	
Thur. 6/11/70	Traffic	Fairport Convention	Mott the Hoople	
Fri. 6/12/70	Procol Harum	Rhinoceros	Seals & Crofts	
Sat. 6/13/70	Procol Harum	Rhinoceros	Seals & Crofts	
Wed. 6/17/70	Laura Nyro	Miles Davis Quartet		

Date	Act 1	Act 2	Act 3	Notes
Thurs. 6/18/70	Laura Nyro	Miles Davis Quartet		
Fri. 6/19/70	Laura Nyro	Miles Davis Quartet		
Sat. 6/20/70	Laura Nyro	Miles Davis Quartet		
Wed. 6/24/70	Ten Years After	Illinoise Speed Press		
Thur. 6/24/70	Ten Years After	Illinoise Speed Press		
Fri. 6/26/70	Chicago	Blodwyn Pig	Jerry Hahn Brotherhood	
Sat. 6/27/70	Chicago	Blodwyn Pig	Jerry Hahn Brotherhood	
Tues. 7/7/70 Tanglewood	Who	Jethro Tull	It's a Beautiful Day	
Thurs. 7/9/70	Grateful Dead	New Riders of the Purple Sage		midnight show
Fri. 7/10/70	Grateful Dead	New Riders of the Purple Sage		midnight show
Sat. 7/11/70	Preservation Hall Jazz Band			8pm show
Sat. 7/11/70	Grateful Dead	New Riders of the Purple Sage		midnight show
Sun. 7/12/70	Preservation Hall Jazz Band			8pm show
Sun. 7/12/70	Grateful Dead	New Riders of the Purple Sage		midnight show
Tues. 7/21/70 Tanglewood	Joe Cocker	John Sebastian	Preservation Hall Jazz Band	program says "Chicago" as 4th group
Fri. 7/24/70	Hot Tuna	Leon Russell	Rig	2 shows
Sat. 7/25/70	Hot Tuna	Leon Russell	Rig	2 shows
Fri. 7/31/70	Grand Funk Railroad	Pacific Gas & Electric	Blood Rock	2 shows
Sat. 8/1/70	Grand Funk Railroad	Pacific Gas & Electric	Blood Rock	2 shows
Wed. 8/5/70	Jethro Tull	Cactus		2 shows
Sat. 8/8/70	Small Faces With Rod Stewart	Blodwyn Pig	Chicken Shack	2 shows
Mon. 8/10/70	Santana	Voices of East Harlem	Ball 'N Jack	2 shows
Tues. 8/11/70	Santana	Voices of East Harlem	Ball 'N Jack	2 shows
Wed. 8/12/70	Santana	Voices of East Harlem	Ball 'N Jack	2 shows
Fri. 8/14/70	Procol Harum	Country Joe McDonald	Toe Fat	2 shows: Seals & Crofts replaced by Toe Fat
Sat. 8/15/70	Procol Harum	Country Joe McDonald	Toe Fat	2 shows: Seals & Crofts replaced by Toe Fat
Tues. 8/18/70 Tanglewood	Santana	Miles Davis	Voices of East Harlem	also: Despess
Fri. 8/21/70	Youngbloods	Blues Image	Tim Harden	2 shows
Sat. /8/22/70	Youngbloods	Blues Image	Tim Harden	2 shows
Fri. 8/28/70	Savoy Brown	Fleetwood Mac	Fairport Convention	
Sat. 8/29/70	Savoy Brown	Fleetwood Mac	Fairport Convention	2 shows
Fri. 9/11/70	Byrds	Delaney and Bonnie & Friends	Great Jones	2 shows
Sat. 9/12/70	Byrds	Delaney and Bonnie & Friends	Great Jones	2 shows
Thur. 9/17/70	Grateful Dead	New Riders of the Purple Sage		
Fri. 9/18/70	Grateful Dead	New Riders of the Purple Sage		Jimi Hendrix dies...
Sat. 9/19/70	Grateful Dead	New Riders of the Purple Sage		
Sun. 9/20/70	Grateful Dead	New Riders of the Purple Sage		
Wed. 9/23/70	Allman Brothers	Van Morrison	Byrds	NET "Welcome to the Fillmore East" taping, also: ShaNaNa, Albert King, Elvin Bishop, Flock
Fri. 9/25/70	Steve Miller Band	Mungo Jerry	Clouds	2 shows
Sat. 9/26/70	Steve Miller Band	Mungo Jerry	Clouds	2 shows
Sun. 9/27/70	Pink Floyd			2 shows produced with Jay K. Hoffman
Fri. 10/2/70	Johnny Winter	Buddy Miles	Tin House	2 shows
Sat. 10/3/70	Johnny Winter	Buddy Miles	Tin House	2 shows
Fri. 10/9/70	John Mayall	Its a Beautiful Day	Flock	2 shows
Sat. 10/10/70	John Mayall	Its a Beautiful Day	Flock	2 shows
Mon. 10/12/70	Rock Relics Auction			
Fri. 10/16/70	B.B. King	Butterfield Blues Band	Elvin Bishop	2 shows
Sat. 10/17/70	B.B. King	Butterfield Blues Band	Elvin Bishop	2 shows
Fri. 10/23/70	Derek & The Dominos	Ball 'N Jack	Humble Pie	2 shows: Humble Pie replaced Juicy Lucy

Date	Headliner	Support	Support	Notes
Sat. 10/24/70	Derek & The Dominos	Ball 'N Jack	Humble Pie	2 shows: Humble Pie replaced Juicy Lucy
Fri. 10/30/70	Lee Michaels	Cactus	Juicy Lucy	2 shows
Sat. 10/3170	Lee Michaels	Cactus	Juicy Lucy	2 shows
Fri. 11/6/70	Albert King	New York Rock & Roll Ensemble	Flying Burrito Brothers	2 shows Mountain cancelled
Sat. 11/7/70	Albert King	New York Rock & Roll Ensemble	Flying Burrito Brothers	2 shows Mountain cancelled
Tues. 11/10/70	Rod Stewart & Small Faces	Black Sabbath		2 shows
Fri. 11/13/70	Frank Zappa & Mothers of Invention	Sha-Na-Na	JF Murphy & Free Flowing Salt	2 shows
Sat. 11/14/70	Frank Zappa & Mothers of Invention	Sha-Na-Na	JF Murphy & Free Flowing Salt	2 shows
Wed. 11/18/70	Traffic	Cat Stevens	Hammer	2 shows
Tues. 11/19/70	Traffic	Cat Stevens	Hammer	2 shows
Fri. 11/20/70	Leon Russell	Elton John	Mckendree Spring	2 shows
Sat. 11/21/70	Leon Russell	Elton John	Mckendree Spring	2 shows
Wed. 11/25/70	Jefferson Airplane	Buddy Guy - Jr. Wells Band		2 shows
Fri. 11/27/70	Jefferson Airplane	Buddy Guy - Jr. Wells Band		2 shows
Sat. 11/28/70	Jefferson Airplane	Buddy Guy - Jr. Wells Band		2 shows
Sun. 11/29/70	Incredible String Band			produced in association With Jay K. Hoffman
Tues. 12/1/70	Virgil Fox			"Richard Torrence presents Heavy Organ"
Fri. 12/4/70	Kinks	Love with Arthur Lee	Quartermass	
Sat. 12/5/70	Kinks	Love with Arthur Lee	Quartermass	
Fri. 12/11/70	Canned Heat	Allman Brothers	Dreams/ Toe Fat	2 shows Toe Fat late shows only
Sat. 12/12/70	Canned Heat	Allman Brothers	Dreams/ Toe Fat	2 shows Toe Fat late shows only
Fri. 12/18/70	Savoy Brown	Poco	Gypsy/Jo Mama	2 shows: Jo Mama performed at late shows only
Sat. 12/19/70	Savoy Brown	Poco	Gypsy/Jo Mama	2 shows: Jo Mama performed at late shows only
Tues. 12/22/70	Laura Nyro	Jackson Brown		
Wed. 12/23/70	Laura Nyro	Jackson Brown		
Thur. 12/24/70	Laura Nyro	Jackson Brown		
Sat. 12/26/70	Mountain	Mylon	David Rea	2 shows
Sun. 12/27/70	Mountain	Mylon	David Rea	
Wed. 12/30/70	Mountain	Mylon	David Rea	
Thur. 12/31/70	Mountain	Mylon	David Rea	2 shows
Fri. 1/8/71	Buddy Miles	Big Brother	Sweetwater	2 shows
Sat. 1/9/71	Buddy Miles	Big Brother	Sweetwater	2 shows
Fri. 1/15/71	Hot Tuna (electric)	Taj Mahal	Brethren	2 shows
Sat. 1/16/71	Hot Tuna (electric)	Taj Mahal	Brethren	2 shows
Fri. 1/22/71	Dave Mason & Cass Elliot	Livingston Taylor	Odetta	2 shows
Sat. 1/23/71	Dave Mason & Cass Elliot	Livingston Taylor	Odetta	2 shows
Mon. 1/25/71	James Taylor	Victoria		2 shows: "Special Charity Performance" benefit
Fri. 1/29/71	Spirit	Blood Rock	Cowboy	2 shows
Sat. 1/30/71	Spirit	Blood Rock	Cowboy	2 shows
Fri. 2/5/71	Steppenwolf	Ten Wheel Drive with Genya Ravan	Luther Allison	2 shows
Sat. 2/6/71	Steppenwolf	Ten Wheel Drive with Genya Ravan	Luther Allison	2 shows
Thur. 2/11/71	Roberta Flack	Taj Mahal	Leon Thomas	
Fri. 2/12/71	Chambers Brothers	Taj Mahal	Spencer Davis & Peter Jameson	
Sat. 2/13/71	Chambers Brothers	Taj Mahal	Spencer Davis & Peter Jameson	
Tues. 2/16/71	Savoy Brown w/ Kim Simmonds	Small Faces with Rod Stewart (special guest)	Grease Band	2 shows

Wed. 2/17/71	Savoy Brown w/ Kim Simmonds	Small Faces with Rod Stewart (special guest)	Grease Band	2 shows
Fri. 2/19/71	Black Sabbath	J. Geils Band	Sir Lord Baltimore	2 shows
Sat. 2/20/71	Black Sabbath	J. Geils Band	Sir Lord Baltimore	2 shows
Fri. 2/26/71	Fleetwood Mac	Van Morrison	Freeway	2 shows
Sat. 2/27/71	Fleetwood Mac	Van Morrison	Freeway	2 shows
Sun. 2/28/71	Gordon Lightfoot	Happy & Artie Traum		
Fri. 3/5/71	Quicksilver Messenger Service	Eric Burdon & War	War	
Sat. 3/6/71	Quicksilver Messenger Service	Eric Burdon & War	War	
Thur. 3/11/71	Johnny Winter	Allman Brothers	Elvin Bishop Group	
Fri. 3/12/71	Johnny Winter	Allman Brothers	Elvin Bishop Group	
Sat. 3/13/71	Johnny Winter	Allman Brothers	Elvin Bishop Group	
Thur. 3/18/71	Astrology Now			
Fri. 3/19/71	Cactus	Humble Pie	Dada	
Sat. 3/20/71	Cactus	Humble Pie	Dada	
Sun. 3/21/71	"Spring for Lowenstein" George Segal, MC Benefit: Theo Bikel, Dick Benjamin, Adolph Green, Dick Bergman, Betty Comden, Ben Gazzara, Barry Grey, Paul Butterfield, Bella Abzug, Tom Lehrer, Mayor John Lindsay, Mitch Miller, Paula Prentiss, Stiller & Meara			
Fri. 3/26/71	Richie Havens	Mark Almond	Paul Siebel/ Michael Grando	Michael Grando (mime) on late show only
Sat. 3/27/71	Richie Havens	Mark Almond	Paul Siebel/ Michael Grando	Michael Grando (mime) on late show only
Thurs. 4/1/71	Santana	Tower of Power	Rahsaan Roland Kirk & Vibration Society	
Fri. 4/2/71	Santana	Tower of Power	Rahsaan Roland Kirk & Vibration Society	
Sat. 4/3/71	Santana	Tower of Power	Rahsaan Roland Kirk & Vibration Society	
Sun. 4/4/71	Howdy Doody Revival with Buffalo Bob Smith			
Mon. 4/5/71	Cactus; Humble Pie	Edgar Winter's White Trash	Tin House	Jethro Tull was headlining and cancelled both
Tues. 4/6/71	Cactus; Humble Pie	Edgar Winter's White Trash	Tin House	Jethro Tull was headlining and cancelled both
Thurs. 4/8/71	Elton John	Sea Train	Wishbone Ash	
Fri. 4/9/71	Elton John	Sea Train	Wishbone Ash	
Sat. 4/10/71	Elton John	Sea Train	Wishbone Ash	
Mon. 4/12/71	Mountain	Mylon	T. Rex	
Tues. 4/13/71	Mountain	Mylon	T. Rex	
Wed. 4/14/71	Mountain	Mylon	T. Rex	
Thur. 4/15/71	Mountain	Mylon	T. Rex	
Fri. 4/16/71	John Mayall	Boz Scaggs	Randall's Island	
Sat. 4/17/71	John Mayall	Boz Scaggs	Randall's Island	
Tues. 4/20/71	Ten Years After	J. Geils Band		
Wed. 4/21/71	Elton John	James Taylor	Richie Havens	
Fri. 4/23/71	Procol Harum	Winter Consort	Teegarden & Van Winkle	
Sat. 4/24/71	Procol Harum	Winter Consort	Teegarden & Van Winkle	
Sun. 4/25/71	Grateful Dead	New Riders of the Purple Sage		
Mon. 4/26/71	Grateful Dead	New Riders of the Purple Sage		
Tues. 4/27/71	Grateful Dead	New Riders of the Purple Sage		
Wed. 4/28/71	Grateful Dead	New Riders of the Purple Sage		
Thur. 4/29/71	Grateful Dead	New Riders of the Purple Sage		
Fri. 4/30/71	Emerson Lake & Palmer	Edgar Winter's White Trash	Curved Air	
Sat. 5/1/71	Emerson Lake & Palmer	Edgar Winter's White Trash	Curved Air	
Tues. 5/4/71	Jethro Tull	Cowboy		
Wed. 5/5/71	Jethro Tull	Cowboy		
Fri. 5/7/71	Poco	Linda Ronstadt	Manhattan Transfer	
Sat. 5/8/71	Poco	Linda Ronstadt	Manhattan Transfer	
Fri. 5/14/71	Delaney & Bonnie	Mott the Hoople	Mandrill	Free was headliner and cancelled
Sat. 5/15/71	Sha Na Na	Mott the Hoople	Mandrill	Free was headliner and cancelled
Thur. 5/20/71	Leon Russell	Taj Mahal	J.F. Murphy & Salt	

Fri. 5/21/71	Leon Russell	Taj Mahal	Donny Hathaway	
Sat. 5/22/71	Leon Russell	Taj Mahal	Donny Hathaway	
Sun. 5/23/71	Leon Russell	Taj Mahal	Donny Hathaway	
Fri. 5/28/71	Lee Michaels	Fanny	Humble Pie was 2nd but appears to have cancelled	
Sat. 5/29/71	Lee Michaels	Fanny	Humble Pie was 2nd but appears to have cancelled	
Sun. 5/30/71	Laura Nyro	Spencer Davis & Peter Jameson		
Sat. 6/5/71	Frank Zappa & The Mothers of Invention	Hampton Grease Band	Head Over Heels	(special guests: John Lennon & Yoko Ono)
Sun. 6/6/71	Frank Zappa & The Mothers of Invention	Hampton Grease Band	Head Over Heels	
Wed. 6/9/71	Byrds	McKendree Spring	Eric Anderson	extra add - late show Elton John

Fri. 6/11/71	Blood Rock	Alice Cooper	Glass Harp	
Sat. 6/12/71	Blood Rock	Alice Cooper	Glass Harp	
Fri. 6/18/71	B.B. King	Moby Grape	Grootna	
Sat. 6/19/71	B.B. King	Moby Grape	Grootna	
Thur. 6/2471	B.B. King	Edgar Winter's White Trash	Albert King	Johnny Winter cancelled
Fri. 6/25/71	Allman Brothers	J. Geils Band	Albert King	
Sat. 6/26/71	Allman Brothers	J. Geils Band	Albert King	
Sun. 6/27/71	Allman Brothers	J. Geils Band	Albert King	Last Show at Fillmore East: Also – Beach Boys, Country Joe, Edgar Winter's White Trash with Rick Derringer, Mountain

INDEX

(Color images indicated in bold)

The concessions stand.

Lobby scene before last concert, Bill Graham and family at right, June 27, 1971.

Leon Russell at Fillmore East, November 20, 1970.

The Band at Fillmore East, May 9, 1969.

Richie Havens at Fillmore East, December 13, 1969.

Mama Cass Elliot at Fillmore East, January 23, 1971.

The crowd milling about outside during the only bomb scare, March 20, 1970. The chaos lasted for a short time, as no bomb was found, and the show continued after only a 45-minute interruption.